WALK THIS WAY

WALK ...THIS WAY

FOREWORD BY MAX LUCADO

An Interactive Guide TO FOLLOWING JESUS

TIM WOODROOF

NAVPRESS

BRINGING TRUTH TO LIFE

P.O. Box 35001, Colorado Springs, Colorado 80935

The Navigators is an international Christian organization. Our mission is to reach, disciple, and equip people to know Christ and to make Him known through successive generations. We envision multitudes of diverse people in the United States and every other nation who have a passionate love for Christ, live a lifestyle of sharing Christ's love, and multiply spiritual laborers among those without Christ.

NavPress is the publishing ministry of The Navigators. NavPress publications help believers learn biblical truth and apply what they learn to their lives and ministries. Our mission is to stimulate spiritual formation among our readers.

Library of Congress Catalog Card Number: 98-41204
ISBN 1-57683-114-0

Cover photo by Tom Francisco/Graphistock

Some of the anecdotal illustrations in this book are true to life and are included with the permission of the persons involved. All other illustrations are composites of real situations, and any resemblance to people living or dead is coincidental.

Unless otherwise identified, all Scripture quotations in this publication are taken from the *HOLY BIBLE: NEW INTERNATIONAL VERSION*® (NIV®). Copyright © 1973, 1978, 1984 by International Bible Society. Used by permission of Zondervan Publishing House. All rights reserved. Other versions used include the *Revised Standard Version Bible* (RSV), copyright © 1946, 1952, 1971, by the Division of Christian Education of the National Council of the Churches of Christ in the USA, used by permission, all rights reserved.

Woodroof, Tim, 1955-
    Walk this way : an interactive guide for following Jesus / Tim Woodroof.
        p. cm.
    Includes bibliographical references.
        ISBN 1-57683-114-0 (pbk.)
        1. Christian life—Biblical teaching. 2. Beatitudes—Study and teaching.
    I. Title.
BV4501.2.W625 1999   98-41204
248.4—dc21   CIP

Printed in the United States of America

1 2 3 4 5 6 7 8 9 10 11 12 13 14 15 / 05 04 03 02 01 00 99 98

FOR A FREE CATALOG OF
NAVPRESS BOOKS & BIBLE STUDIES,
CALL 1-800-366-7788 (USA)
OR 1-416-499-4615 (CANADA)

To
Sarah,
James,
and
Jonathan
who, more than others,
know how far from the Beatitudes
their father lives
but love him anyway.
And
to Julie
who, far more than most,
makes Beatitude living look possible.
I love you.

Acknowledgments

Writing only looks like a solitary endeavor. In fact, it's a team sport. So I'd like to introduce some of the other people who made this book possible—the other members of my writing team.

My brothers and sisters at the Westside Church in Beaverton, Oregon, allowed me to preach through the Beatitudes twice—once at the beginning of my ministry with them (in 1990) and once at the close of our time together (in 1997). This book flows from that preaching experience. Without their listening ears and reflective comments, there wouldn't be a book.

In the summer of 1997, my family moved to Searcy, Arkansas—where living was cheap and my parents had a house for rent—so I could devote myself to writing for a year. Our house in Portland sold but failed to close. Without a steady income, we found ourselves saddled with a mortgage 2,500 miles away. Times got desperate.

During the next ten months, various friends stepped forward to help us survive financially. Their selfless and steady support made writing possible. While I make my living with words, I don't have the words to express my gratitude for their help. I do want you to meet them, however, and know their role in putting this book in your hands. Thank you to Chris and Trudi Sherk, Allen and Terry Figley, Rusty and Nancy Meadows, Dan and Alisa Davidson, C. E. and Melody Ransom, Sam and Cathie Shultz, David and Wilma Pace, Ron and Janyth Baker, and Lowell and Nancy Myers.

Much of the actual writing occurred in a small conference room in the library of Harding University. The staff there was unfailingly gracious and helpful. My thanks to Ann, Ann, Jan, and Henry.

A number of people read through the manuscript, offering both encouragement and helpful criticism. Of course, I first inflict all my writing on my wife—thanks, Julie. I'm also blessed with preaching buddies whose judgment I trust. Kelly Carter, Rick Atchley,

Mike Cope, and (especially) Ron Stump assured me that these words made sense and might actually help other people follow Jesus more closely. My mom and dad, Jim and Louine Woodroof, caught more grammatical errors in the manuscript than I would care to admit.

I invited Ross Cochran, Jim Carr, Cathie Shultz, Nick Kennedy, and Bruce McLarty to meet with me weekly to discuss their reactions to the manuscript. I bought them coffee for the privilege of picking their brains. Their comments made a real difference in the shape and tone of this book. Thank you!

The "Top Ten" lists were a feature I wanted to include in this book but was unable to develop personally (I'm humor-impaired). Dennis Lynn, Monty Moreland, and Vern Meaders, on the other hand, do not suffer from my disability. Their inventiveness and strange twists of thinking are responsible for whatever fun you derive from the Top Ten lists.

For Max Lucado to write the Foreword to this book is a great honor. I have long read and benefited from his books. Thank you, Max, for taking the time to endorse this effort. It means a lot to me.

Finally, a word of thanks to NavPress for their support of this project. Sue Geiman and Brad Lewis (my editor) saw the potential for this new format and helped me set a higher standard in my writing. The "look and feel" of this book is largely a result of their vision.

I hope this book is good for you. On behalf of this whole team, I want you to know that what we've done together has been for you. Accept this as an expression of our desire to minister to you. We hope it makes a difference in your life.

TIM WOODROOF

Foreword

The computer age has given rise to a new breed of geniuses—techies. The problem is, they don't always know how to tell us what to do. They spout terms like software, megabytes, and hard drive. Our response is, "Huh?"

Long before computers had techies, the church had theologians. Again the problem is, they don't always know how to tell us what to do. They spout terms like predestination, sanctification, and propitiation. Our response? We tilt our heads and say, "What?"

Every so often, however, a techie makes the effort to make it simple and we all benefit.

And every so often, a theologian does the same. Tim Woodroof has done exactly that. He is clear without being shallow. The teaching is nutritious without being bland. His ideas are just high enough to stretch you, but not so lofty as to discourage you.

I'm hopeful that this work of Tim's is the first of many. I'm equally hopeful that you, the reader, will be one of thousands blessed by his instruction. Thanks, Tim, for placing the cookies on the lower shelf.

Maybe I'll find somebody to do the same for me and my computer.

Max Lucado

Preface

A Brief Word About Reading This Book

The premise of the book you hold in your hands is that if we're serious about discipleship, we need an instruction manual for following Jesus. The Beatitudes, spoken by Jesus to his first disciples, come closer to being a guide for following him than anything else I can think of. Together, we'll explore what the Beatitudes teach about following Jesus.

This book is not *the* instruction manual—it's simply a guide that points you toward it. Think of it as a frame, rather than the picture. The wrapping, not the gift. The Beatitudes themselves are the valuable part of the package. This book is simply a setting (whether of gold or some baser metal, you must judge) designed to show off the Beatitudes in all their luster and loveliness.

WHO SHOULD READ THIS BOOK

I've tried to make this book accessible to a wide range of readers. The manuscript has been read by seminary professors, ministers, church members, students, and even my thirteen-year-old daughter (although I had to threaten her allowance once or twice to provide extra motivation). People of various ages and educations have helped me hone the writing. Although I assume you have some familiarity with the Bible, you don't have to be able to quote extensive passages from Jeremiah to get the point of this book. As a minister, I hope my fellow pastors find material here for the pulpit. As someone who loves the church, I pray that people in the pew will enjoy and benefit from what I've written.

Most of all, I've written with new Christians in mind—those who bring great eagerness to the process of becoming disciples but don't know exactly where to begin. If you're a new Christian (or you know a new Christian), this book is for you.

To make good use of this book, you need three qualifications:

1. You must be serious about discipleship—or at least seriously curious. Those who are content with a casual Christianity, who want nothing more than to be left alone, won't find much comfort here. (Of course, people like that are rarely standing in a Christian bookstore, scanning the preface of a book about discipleship!)

2. You must have faith that God wouldn't leave us without directions for becoming disciples. While there are many important things in our lives for which we have no instructions, discipleship is *too important* to lack directions. If you haven't found the manual for following Jesus yet, you must believe that it exists if you want to make much use of this book.

3. You must possess an openness to the notion that it's not *understanding* the instructions that is difficult, but putting them into consistent *practice*. You're not done with the Beatitudes when you finish this book. Actually, the Beatitudes aren't done with you. Reading is just the beginning—the real work is translating what you learn into how you live.

PREVIEW OF FEATURES

The leap from theory to practice can be a long one. We all need a little shove now and then to move from being "hearers only" to "doers of the word" (to borrow the language of a biblical writer named James). As you read, you'll come across some unique features—interactive elements I've included to push you toward applying what you're learning.

Mixed throughout the main text of each chapter are statistics, quotes, and other items that might seem only remotely related to the Beatitudes. This is partly for fun, to make the book more inviting. But these elements are also touchstones to our culture. Being a disciple means understanding enough of our culture to live out Jesus' instructions within that culture. According to the record we have of Jesus' public life, that's exactly what he did.

Following each Beatitude discussion is a "Top Ten" list to underscore the point of the chapter in a lighter way. As you enjoy these lists, don't forget to laugh at yourself— you've probably been guilty of one of the "Top Ten Stupid

Penance Tricks" or experienced one of the "Top Ten Unexpected Results of Hungering for Righteousness."

Each chapter also includes a portrait of a relatively famous person (Mother Teresa, John Newton, Chuck Colson) who has exemplified that Beatitude. The idea is to paint a picture of what each Beatitude looks like when lived out by a real person. Seeing someone else put a Beatitude into practice encourages us to do the same.

Finally, three "guides" are included with each chapter—one for further study, one for discussion, and one for application.

"Thinking It Through" is a daily study guide that builds on the chapters by pointing you back to Scripture. Spend a few minutes each day looking at appropriate texts, reflecting on biblical teachings, and deepening your understanding of each Beatitude. Just reading this book is like looking over my shoulder while I'm digging into the Bible. It's important for you to do some digging of your own.

"Talking It Over" is a discussion guide that takes the material you've read and measures a biblical character by that standard. The idea is to meet with a few friends to chat about Nebuchadnezzar and how he learned to be poor in spirit, or Jeremiah and the persecutions he endured. These discussion guides will help a group of readers talk about what they're learning and encourage each other to apply that knowledge.

Finally, the goal of "Living It Out" is to help you implement what you're learning. You'll be "prescribed" a task or two to help make each Beatitude more real. Often, you'll find a prayer to repeat in your own quiet time. You may be asked to do something that requires another person—share a failing, offer an apology, lend a helping hand. Here, *you* are the one who is being asked to embody the Beatitudes. No doubt, these tangible expressions of discipleship will be the most difficult part of this book. I pray that you won't stop with the words, that you'll become a "doer" of what you know.

ALL TOGETHER NOW

This book is best read in the context of a community. Several people reading together will make for a more powerful encounter with the Beatitudes than one person reading alone. These ideas have to be talked about and argued over and bounced back and forth to truly be appreciated. I've supplied some tools to encourage reading in groups. But you must supply the group.

Let me suggest two specific ways this can be done.

Pull together a few interested readers and meet weekly to discuss a chapter. A Sunday school class, a young married couples' group, a prayer breakfast, a circle of friends—any collection of people interested in spiritual things will do. Begin with prayer and have someone in the group summarize the main points of the chapter. Work through the "Talking It Over" segment.

Find ways to encourage each other to apply what you've studied.

Another idea is to pair a new Christian with an older, more mature believer. If you've walked with Jesus for a while and you know someone who is just beginning his or her life in Christ, buy two copies of this book, give one to your friend, and ask this new Christian to meet you for breakfast once a week. Talk about what you're learning. Share experiences from your own successes and failures. Take the time to guide someone else as they attempt to follow Jesus. It's the single best investment of time and energy you can make for the kingdom—and in your own spiritual growth.

If *you* are the new Christian, be bold! Buy two copies of the book. Find someone whose faith you admire, a person you respect and want to know better. Give that person one copy and keep the other. Ask him or her to meet with you and discuss the Beatitudes for the next few months.

Offer to pay for the coffee! You'll only be out a few dollars and a little time, but the return on your investment will be eternal.

KILLING US SOFTLY

Roberta Flack climbed the pop charts in 1973 with a song entitled, "Killing Me Softly." It is a ballad about a girl who goes to a concert because she is told the singer "sings a good song." But she is shocked to discover just how powerful and cutting his songs are. His words embarrass her. They make her wonder if he has been reading her letters. She feels that he is exposing every dark secret of her life while the rest of the crowd listens in. As Roberta croons the chorus, we hear the girl mourn that this singer is "killing me softly with his song."

Jesus does that with the Beatitudes. He kills us softly.

We come to listen because we hear that Jesus sings a good song. He has a reputation for wisdom and genuine spirituality. But, in coming to Jesus, we get more than we bargained for. There, in front of God and everyone, Jesus tells the story of our lives out loud. He shows the pettiness of our morality, the shallowness of our character, the carelessness of our spirituality. We come to Jesus self-satisfied and find ourselves undone by his words. We feel naked and vulnerable as he turns over every rock and exposes things in us we'd rather keep hidden.

Then—once we get past the embarrassment, once we stop feeling like ugly ducklings—something wonderful begins to happen. We discover a genuine power in his words. They create a transforming tension within us.

Yes, the Beatitudes kill us softly. But what they take away, they more than restore. There's far more than judgment here—they paint a portrait of a new kind of living that transcends anything we've ever known. While the Beatitudes convict us of low living, they also entice us with a higher vision of what life can be. Somewhere between the shame we feel and the ideal we can't reach alone lies a powerful motivation to change — to leave behind compromised living and to pursue the goal that Jesus set out on the mountainside so long ago.

Even as he is killing us softly, Jesus is busy raising us back to life.

Welcome to the Beatitudes — the instruction manual for following Jesus.

CHAPTER ONE

The Illustrated DISCIPLE

f I close my eyes, I can still see his upturned face.

Scott was a new Christian. Fresh from alcohol and cynicism, he'd recently turned to Christ for answers. Each Sunday, he sat with open Bible and eager expression, waiting for me to teach him the ABCs of following Jesus. And each Sunday, he left disappointed. He wouldn't say it in words. But week after week, I watched his eyes glaze over, his Bible slowly close, and the expectant expression fade from his face.

Oh, I had the MNOs of discipleship down cold. I could teach Scott the XYZs. I could expound on the minor prophets and discuss differing views on the Second Coming.

But somewhere along the way, I'd forgotten what it was like to be a "newbie" in Christ . . . how daunting discipleship could seem . . . how overwhelming it all could be.

Then one Sunday I began a series on the Beatitudes. I watched Scott listen—riveted to these simple words from Jesus. I saw him writing frantically in the margin of his Bible, whispering urgently to his wife, sitting quietly in his seat long after we dismissed. He bought the tapes. He came by the office to ask questions. He wanted a reading list.

Call me slow. But it took me a while to realize that Scott—so eager to grow in Christ, so willing to follow

NEWBIE
A newcomer, especially an inexperienced user of the Internet or of computers in general.
—Webster's Collegiate Dictionary

where Jesus would lead—didn't know where to begin. Until he heard the Beatitudes.

A PLACE TO START

We're drowning in words about following Jesus. Walk into a Christian bookstore and chances are you'll feel swamped. The flood of information about discipleship coming from books, pulpits, Christian television, and radio is astounding . . . and bewildering. But how many of these words can be trusted? How many of these words are really necessary? And just how many of these words must we read before we really learn?

In the face of this informational tidal wave, many Christians (new and old) want to shout some simple questions: "Where do I start as a disciple of Jesus?" "What steps are necessary to become what he wants me to be?" "Are there any straightforward instructions on following Jesus?"

What we need is a guide for discipleship—something

> **THE MAKING OF MANY BOOKS**
> More than 25,000 new religious books have been published in the last ten years. More than 155 million copies of books related to religion were bought by Americans in 1995.
> —Publisher's Weekly

short, sweet, and to the point. We need something to help us troubleshoot our lives when things go wrong, something we can review over the years to get back in touch with the basics.

But my guess is that you didn't get one when you became a Christian. It's not that you mislaid it along the way or ran it through the wash. They never gave you one. How do you like that? The most important commitment of your life and no user's manual to go along with it!

We have instruction manuals and guidebooks for everything—except the things we need them for most. I have a booklet filled with detailed directions for unstopping my garbage disposal. But no one gave me an instruction manual that tells me how to build character in my kids. I'd gladly trade the manual about my lawnmower or the one that came with my washing machine for some simple directions on what to say

> **FOREVER 12:00**
> It's estimated that between 20 percent and 35 percent of VCR owners don't know how to set the digital clocks on their machines.
> — Bradley University

to a wife whose feelings I've wounded. I'd be willing to have my VCR flash "12:00" for the rest of its natural life if I could exchange its instruction booklet for clear instructions on what to do with a friendship that's gone sour or a neighbor who won't mow his yard or in-laws who stay too long.

As it is, I have a drawer full of instruction manuals for things I couldn't care less about and a life full of things I care about with no instructions to go with them.

It's at this point in the discussion that some well-meaning Christian throws a Bible at us and says, "Here, just read this!" Hmmm . . . thanks for the sentiment, but that's not very helpful. I open my Bible of more than a thousand pages and feel lost. How much do I need to master before I can figure out the basics? Do I need to know about the tabernacle or decipher Revelation or grasp the finer points of redemptive history before I can walk confidently in the footsteps of Jesus? The Bible is wonderful, but it's long. It has rich nuggets about following Jesus, but you have to do a lot of digging to get to the gold.

Forgive me for insisting I need something shorter, something more direct and to the point. Give me something I can get my arms around *right now*. Don't make me start with Leviticus and Ezekiel and Hebrews to find out how to be the disciple God wants me to be. Give me something that covers the basics, something simple and specific, something I can write on a three-by-five index card.

Do that for me, and maybe — just maybe — I can begin to be a disciple of Jesus.

JESUS, THE APOSTLES, AND FIRST WORDS

[Jesus] went up on a mountainside and sat down. His disciples came to him, and he began to teach them. . . .
—MATTHEW 5:1-2

The men Jesus chose as disciples sat around him with expectant expressions. Peter. John and James. Thomas. Andrew. Twelve of them altogether. They came from all walks of life. They brought all kinds of baggage. And they didn't have any more clue than the rest of us.

Just like us, they met Jesus and knew there was something special about him. They put their faith in him — faith enough to leave their old lives behind and begin new lives as followers of the prophet from Nazareth.

According to the gospel accounts, Jesus collected these individuals by wandering around Galilee, issuing the invitation, "Follow me." Peter and Andrew were fishing out in a boat when Jesus called over the water, "Follow me and I will make you fishers of men." The same challenge went out to James and John, and to Matthew Levi.

One by one, the disciples heard, left, and followed.

But they didn't know what they were doing. These were fishermen, not theologians. They were sincere, earnest Jews who went to the synagogue on the Sabbath and tried to make it to Jerusalem for the Passover. But they hadn't been to seminary. They hadn't poured over biblical texts preparing themselves to be followers of the Messiah. These were ordinary men with more expertise in boats and tax tables than in the ways of God.

If you think about it, Peter had to start somewhere. John had to learn the basics somehow. The apostles weren't popped out of a mold — ready-made and fully formed. Like us, they had to learn the ABCs of following Jesus.

They needed an instruction manual as badly as we do.

Jesus knew what they needed, of

FISH IN THE SEA OF GALILEE
Damselfish, catfish, barbels, mouthbreeders (don't ask!), and (my personal favorite) scaleless blennies.
—Encyclopaedia Brittanica

UNLUCKY 13
In the past, 12 was considered a perfect number, signifying harmony and completeness (like 7 and 40). But 13, in contrast, represented confusion and chaos. What really killed 13, however, was when someone calculated that at the Last Supper, Judas the Betrayer was the thirteenth person at the table.
—The Straight Dope

FIRST WORDS
Infants speak their first word at twelve to fourteen months. Usually that word is a simple label for people, objects, or actions, such as "mommy," "go," or "milk." One of my son's first sentences: "I'm a vicious rhino."

course. He wanted his first words to them to meet that need. He'd prepared a guide of sorts to give them. But apparently it was important for these instructions to be delivered all at once. So Jesus waited until the first disciples were all together before telling them the basics about the business of being his followers.

If you read Matthew's and Luke's accounts, you'll hear a strange silence settle over the story between the call to follow and the Beatitudes. From their initial invitation until the entire group is gathered on a hillside in Galilee, there are no words just for the disciples. Instead Jesus spoke to a leper, the Pharisees, a paralytic, a critic or two, and a man with a shriveled hand. But, to the disciples, he uttered not a word.[1] It's as if Jesus avoided speaking to his chosen followers until all were present and he could address the entire group.

His opportunity came when he gathered the disciples on a mountainside.[2] Seating them around himself, Jesus spoke to the group for the first time. I like the way the *New International Version* translates it: "He *began* to teach them. . . ."[3]

First words are important. We proudly take note of the first words spoken by our children. The opening sentence of a book has greater significance than one tucked away on page 176. We invest inaugural addresses and commencement exercises with special significance.

Perhaps we should listen with extreme care to the first words of Jesus to his assembled disciples. These are the words that Jesus had been saving for just this moment, the words that would "baptize" these spiritual novices and initiate them into Christ's inner circle. They are defining words, christening words, formative words.

We call them the Beatitudes. But Jesus might call them his instruction manual for building disciples.

"Blessed are the poor in spirit,
  for theirs is the kingdom of heaven.
Blessed are those who mourn,
  for they will be comforted.
Blessed are the meek, for they
  will inherit the earth.
Blessed are those who hunger
  and thirst for righteousness,
  for they will be filled.
Blessed are the merciful,
  for they will be shown mercy.
Blessed are the pure in heart,
  for they will see God.
Blessed are the peacemakers,
  for they will be called sons
  of God.
Blessed are those who are persecuted because of righteousness, for theirs is the kingdom of heaven."[4]

Eight succinct sentences. Ninety-six simple words. Nothing you have to look up in a dictionary. Nothing that requires a graduate degree to understand. These lines are lean, spare, elegant. There's no fat, no surplus here. They flow like poetry and cut like a knife.

We assume that words came easily to Jesus — spontaneously, effortlessly, just the right word for the right occasion. But not these words. There's nothing extemporaneous about the Beatitudes. He must have planned this first meeting with his disciples for years. I can see him rehearsing these words while still in the carpentry shop at Nazareth: "Peter, John, guys . . . I have something to tell you." Perhaps he honed this speech while sharpening his saws and chisels. I don't think these words were made up on the spot. Jesus knew exactly what he wanted to tell these men long before he called them together.

And what did he want to tell them? You might expect him to introduce himself.

Hello. My name is Jesus. I'm the Son of God, the Alpha and the Omega, the bright and morning star. You may have read about me in the writings of Moses and the prophets.

Or you'd think he might start by giving them his mission statement: "I have come to seek and to save the lost." Or by letting them know what their mission was to be: "You are to be my witnesses." It wouldn't surprise us if he'd begun by telling them stories of the kingdom of heaven or giving them a preview of what the next three years would be like.

Instead, Jesus talked to his disciples not about himself, not about the mission, not about the kingdom. He talked to them about them. His first words described the characteristics he would look for in those who followed him. They described the kind of people he wanted his followers to become. They defined what it meant to be his disciple.

Now, *that's* interesting. If these words were intentionally foundational for his first disciples, perhaps they're intended to be foundational for us as well. If they defined the followers of Jesus in the first century, maybe they do the same for followers of Jesus in the twenty-first century.

What we have in the Beatitudes is an instruction manual for discipleship — one that applies to all Christians. Eight basic directions for growing up in Christ. Eight steps to the heart of God. Eight powerful and compelling portraits of life lived as a follower of Jesus. The essence of discipleship in a thimble. The heart of Christianity in a paragraph that can be written on a postcard.

YOU GET WHAT YOU PAY FOR

The only thing worse than having no instructions is being stuck with *bad* instructions. It's frustrating enough when you get faulty directions about trivial things. Try putting together a Christmas toy using an instruction manual written by someone whose first language isn't English: "Please to put plastic device green into snapping-on slot." That's really irritating.

Toys are one thing. But with some things there's no room for unclear or faulty instructions. We won't tolerate ambiguous directions on prescription bottles. Parachutes must come with *flawless* instructions. We have no patience with haphazard advice about caring for our children.

Yet Christians seem remarkably casual about the quality of instruction they receive for discipleship. Frequently, we're thrown into discipleship with little or no direction—the "sink or swim" school of disciplemaking. When we do receive instruction, it's often vague and unthinking—the "ignorance loves company" method of disciplemaking. Worst of all, some of the advice we're handed about discipleship is just plain wrong.

But why should that surprise us? Bad advice about discipleship has never been in short supply.

Some people in the first century insisted, "You must be circumcised and obey the law of Moses to be a true disciple." That sounded good (except the circumcision part!) and persuaded many a Gentile Christian to become an observant Jew. But the apostle Paul called this advice a perversion of the gospel.[5] You don't become the disciple Jesus wants you to be by cutting off parts of your anatomy and refusing to eat certain foods. Bad advice.

In the second century, a fellow by the name of Montanus told people they couldn't marry, had to take a vow of poverty, fast to the point of starvation, and seek martyrdom at every opportunity to be a real disciple of Jesus. Amazingly, he won enough followers to split churches throughout the Mediterranean world for the next 300 years. But he was wrong. Ascetics don't have a corner on the salvation market. He was handing out bad instructions about discipleship.

In the sixteenth century, a monk by the name of Tetzel said that if you made a sizable contribution to the building of St. Peter's Basilica in Rome, the pope would permit you to engage in the sin of your choice and still remain a disciple in good standing. The massively expensive cathedral was built from the donations of people who listened to and believed what Tetzel said about discipleship. But Tetzel was wrong. That's not how disciples act. That's bad advice about how to follow Jesus.

Bad advice about discipleship is still abundant today.

There are people who insist that discipleship depends on what position you hold on the millennium or whether you speak in tongues or which political party you belong to. They'll tell you that the way to discipleship is secret or obscure or esoteric. They'll make you jump through hoops and walk on coals and embark on quests for the Holy Grail. They'll try to convince you that discipleship is about conformity or doctrinal correctness or moral perfection. They'll ask you to focus on behaviors or positions or rituals. They'll make instructions about discipleship complicated and detailed and exhaustive.

They'll be very sincere, very earnest, and very wrong.

Not everything people say about discipleship is helpful. Not everything we're told about following Jesus is worth listening to. Not every word on the subject is the gospel truth. So be careful. There's a lot of bad advice out there. Insist on the genuine article. Make sure your instruction manual reads, "Written in heaven." Accept no substitutes.

RIGHT FROM THE MASTER'S MOUTH

As it happens, Jesus himself has something to say about becoming his disciple. Above the hubbub of the religious pied pipers, we can hear his quiet words—if we listen carefully.

The Beatitudes are Christ's instruction manual for building a disciple. In them, he describes eight steps to becoming the Christian you always wanted to be. They won't make your hair grow back or help you take off that extra twenty pounds. They won't improve your golf handicap or make you a safer driver. They won't even teach you how to program your VCR.

What they will do is change your life. They'll teach you the most important skills for facing your most challenging spiritual problem—yourself. They'll identify the attitudes necessary for living in the presence of God. They'll educate you in the ways disciples live and deal with other people. They'll help you manage your most intimate relationships.

These aren't just thoughtless soundbites, tossed off by Jesus to warm up his audience before getting to the meat of his sermon. These are the foundation points—key characteristics—for people who want to walk in his footsteps. With eight sure strokes, Jesus paints the portrait of a true believer.

That's what Jesus was doing on the mountainside that day. He was presenting an instruction manual for disciples. Before things got too hectic, before the Pharisees got their noses out of joint, before the mobs began to press and make their demands, Jesus took a few moments to lay out the ground rules for those who wanted to follow him.

Because Matthew records these words, we can look over the shoulders of the Twelve and listen in as Jesus tells them about life as a disciple. As we eavesdrop on this conversation, we learn not just who *they* were to become but who God wants *us* to become. The words Jesus spoke so long ago become marching orders for those of us who want to be his modern-day followers.

These eight Beatitudes—spoken on a desert mountainside in an isolated portion of an obscure country by a callous-handed carpenter to a group of nobodies—have impacted more people than any words ever spoken. What Jesus taught that day has instructed and trained and shaped more lives than any book ever written. This one paragraph has chaffed and challenged and changed individuals for 2,000 years.

But be warned: Change never comes easily. Transformation always involves struggle. If you're looking for eight bloodless steps to eternal bliss, this isn't the place to find them. Don't expect results if you skip over the hard parts and practice the rest only occasionally. But if you apply yourself to what Jesus says here, to following his instructions carefully and implementing them consistently, I guarantee God will use these Beatitudes to build himself a disciple.

The Beatitudes can change your life. The question is not whether they have the power to change you. The question is: Do they have your permission?

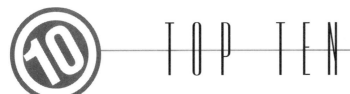

TOP TEN . . .

TOP TEN REASONS TO STUDY THE BEATITUDES

10. There are only eight of 'em!

9. What else can you study that promises heaven and earth?

8. There's not a single "Thou shalt not" in the lot!

7. Learn to impress religious friends with public prayers and personal piety. No, wait! That's one of the reasons for studying the *Pharisees*. Sorry.

6. Learn enough about the subject of mercy that you can destroy anyone in a discussion of the topic.

5. They're more interesting than Leviticus.

4. Consider it a way of cramming for the *real* final exam.

3. They're something to think about while brushing your teeth.

2. They are guaranteed to change your life or your money back.

And the **#1** reason to study the Beatitudes:

It beats memorizing the Ten Commandments!

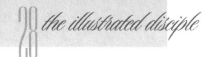

THE STORY OF...

Jesus

THE BEATITUDES IN THE FLESH

What famous person is a model for the Beatitudes as a whole? I can think of only one person whose life can bear up under that sort of examination.

Jesus is talking about us in the Beatitudes—he's describing who we should be. But, in a very real way, we find Jesus in the Beatitudes. Listen carefully and you'll hear a summary of Christ's character. The Beatitudes *are* Jesus, a portrait of our Master drawn in nouns and verbs.

It doesn't take long to understand that Jesus isn't just giving us pious principles, pie-in-the-sky precepts. In reality, he's describing himself. We listen to him talk about the meek, the hungry, the pure, and the persecuted—and we realize that Jesus is actually talking about himself.

How close to his presence we come in reading these few brief verses! The Beatitudes transport us back to a hillside in Galilee to sit with tax collectors and Pharisees, prostitutes and merchants as they listened to the Rabbi from Nazareth. We hear Christ with an immediacy and a clarity that belies the centuries standing between us. For a few brief moments, our ears become eyes.

In the chart on the following page I've paired some verses about Jesus with a listing of the Beatitudes. Spend some time meditating on the notion that, in studying the Beatitudes, you're really getting to know Jesus better.

Keep the character of Christ in the back of your mind as you continue reading this book. View this not just as an exercise in becoming a better disciple but as a chance to know Christ better. The Beatitudes will sharpen your understanding of Jesus. They'll lend detail to the lines of his life and the shadings of his personality.

BEATITUDE	HOW JESUS EXEMPLIFIES THE BEATITUDE
Blessed are the poor in spirit	For you know the grace of our Lord Jesus Christ, that though he was rich, yet for your sakes he became poor, so that you through his poverty might become rich. (2 Corinthians 8:9)
Blessed are those who mourn	He was a man of sorrows, and familiar with suffering. (Isaiah 53:3)
Blessed are the meek	"Take my yoke upon you and learn from me, for I am gentle and humble in heart, and you will find rest for your souls." (Matthew 11:29)
Blessed are those who hunger and thirst for righteousness	"My food," said Jesus, "is to do the will of him who sent me and to finish his work." (John 4:34)
Blessed are the merciful	"But go and learn what this means: 'I desire mercy, not sacrifice.' For I have not come to call the righteous, but sinners." (Matthew 9:13)
Blessed are the pure in heart	Fix your thoughts on Jesus, the apostle and high priest whom we confess. . . . Such a high priest meets our need—one who is holy, blameless, pure, set apart from sinners, exalted above the heavens. (Hebrews 3:1; 7:26)
Blessed are the peacemakers	For he himself is our peace, who has made the two one. . . . He came and preached peace to you who were far away and peace to those who were near. (Ephesians 2:14,17)
Blessed are the persecuted	He was oppressed and afflicted, yet he did not open his mouth; he was led like a lamb to the slaughter, and as a sheep before her shearers is silent, so he did not open his mouth. (Isaiah 53:7)

THINKING IT THROUGH

MONDAY

I suggest in this chapter that the Beatitudes may be the first words Jesus spoke to the whole group of disciples. Let's look at the evidence for this.

- Read Matthew 4:18–5:3 and Luke 5:1–6:20. Each of these begins with the call of Peter and Andrew and ends with the first Beatitude. Between these two events, does Jesus say anything to the entire group? Who does Jesus speak with in this interval? Make a list.

- What are the first words in Mark and John addressed to the disciples as a group? What significance do these statements have for discipleship?

- Back to the Beatitudes. Write out your responses to the following questions: If these are the first words Jesus spoke to his disciples, does that lend any special importance to them? If Jesus is describing the kind of people he wants them to become, should that serve as a guide for us as we try to follow Jesus today?

TUESDAY

I call the Beatitudes Christ's instruction manual on discipleship. Finding such a thing in the Bible is not uncommon. In fact, several other instruction manuals addressing different issues and serving different purposes are scattered throughout Scripture. Read the following passages and write down: (1) what the instructions were about, and (2) the circumstances the instructions were given in.

- Exodus 12:1-20
- Skim through Exodus 25:8–31:18
- Leviticus 16:1-34
- Read Proverbs 1:1-6 and consider the possibility that the entire book of Proverbs is really an extended instruction manual.
- Read 1 Timothy 3:14-15. Aren't both of Paul's letters to Timothy simply instructions given by an older preacher to a younger one?

WEDNESDAY

Review the study you did yesterday, then think about the following statements.

- This list identifies traits found in instructions. How are these demonstrated by the instructions you read yesterday?
  1. Good instructions usually add up to "one thing," something you can write on an index card.
  2. Instructions are given by people who know what they're talking about.
  3. Instructions are given to people who have a need to know.
  4. Instructions are called for by the circumstances people find themselves in.
  5. Instructions are often given in lists and are sequenced.
- Now think about the Beatitudes. How do these ideas apply to this group of sayings? Who gives and who receives these instructions? What were the circumstances when the Beatitudes were given? What was their purpose?
- Given what you've just studied, do you think it's reasonable to call the Beatitudes an "instruction manual for discipleship"?

THURSDAY

Bad advice about discipleship has never been in short supply. Not everything people say about discipleship is helpful. Read the following passages and write out the bad advice you find there. How is that advice countered?

- Acts 15:5
- Romans 3:7-8
- 1 Corinthians 1:12; 15:12-14,32
- 2 Corinthians 10:10
- Galatians 6:12-13
- Colossians 2:21
- 1 Timothy 4:1-3
- Jude 4

FRIDAY

Each of the Beatitudes begins with the word "blessed." (In fact, "beatitude" comes from the Latin word for "blessed.") Some writers believe this word means "happy." In a certain sense, it does. But the "blessedness" Jesus speaks of here goes deeper than a good giggle or an emotional high. Read the following passages and think about what this word means.

- Genesis 1:22; 9:1; 24:35-36; 35:9-12
- Exodus 20:11
- Deuteronomy 7:12-15
- Job 5:17
- Psalm 1:1-3
- Matthew 11:2-6; 13:14-17; 16:15-19
- John 20:29
- Ephesians 1:3

What's the most important lesson you learned this week through your study?

TALKING IT OVER

TEXT: EXODUS 19:20–20:20

WARM-UP:

Are you one of those people who actually *reads* instruction manuals or would you rather "figure it out" as you go? (Go around the group and have everyone 'fess up.) One or two of you also might share your worst experience as a result of *not* reading directions.

Whether we like them or not, God seems to be fond of instruction manuals. The most famous set of instructions in the Bible has to be the Ten Commandments, found in Exodus 20. Would one of you volunteer to read Exodus 20:1-17?

DISCUSSION:

1. First, some general questions for you to answer: Who is speaking? Who is the intended audience? Why is this list given? What is its purpose? What are the circumstances? (Read Exodus 19:3-6 for a hint.)
2. *Reading* instructions and *following* them are two different things. The Israelites knew how God wanted them to behave. They just had problems following God's directions. Match up the people with the particular commandment they ignored. (See the chart on the next page. You can read the indicated passages if you need a hint.)
3. Talk about some of the similarities you see between the Ten Commandments and the Beatitudes: setting, purpose, speaker, listeners, effect.
4. Does Matthew want us to think about Jesus as "another Moses," delivering a new "law" from the mountain? If so, what importance does this give to the Beatitudes?

APPLICATION:

1. In your walk with Jesus, have you discovered any instructions to guide you? Or are you just figuring it out as you go? Most of us don't get much specific direction for being disciples. How have you found that frustrating?

2. Have you ever thought about the Beatitudes as an instruction manual for disciples of Jesus? Has this study changed the way you look at the Beatitudes?
3. Like the Israelites, we're *familiar* with God's directions—we just don't *follow* them very well. Would it make any difference in your life if you began each day with a commitment to live by the Beatitudes? How?
4. Which of the Beatitudes is your undoing? Which one do you have the hardest time honoring?

COOL DOWN:

Having instructions doesn't do much good if there's no commitment to follow them. Can you make a commitment to the other members of the group to read the Beatitudes each day this week and try to put them into practice?

The "Living It Out" section includes a prayer. Pray this together as a group as you conclude this session.

BIBLE CHARACTER	COMMANDMENT
A man gathering wood (Numbers 15:32-36)	No other gods
Some of Paul's enemies (Romans 3:8)	No idols
David (2 Samuel 11:1-4)	Don't lie in God's name
Ahab (1 Kings 21:1-4)	Remember the Sabbath
Judas (John 12:6)	Honor father and mother
The Israelites (2 Kings 17:12-17)	No murder
Saul (1 Samuel 19:6,10)	No adultery
Cain's transgression (Genesis 4:8)	No stealing
Solomon (1 Kings 11:4-5)	No false testimony
Absalom (2 Samuel 16:21-22)	No coveting

LIVING IT OUT

Do you know how to eat an elephant? One bite at a time.

Do you know how to become a disciple of Jesus? One step at a time. But having a place to start, knowing where to begin, is vital. That first step can be a doozy if you're not careful!

Discipleship has to start somewhere. Why not begin your walk with Jesus where Jesus asked the Twelve to begin—with the Beatitudes? If you want to do that, memorize the Beatitudes this week. Write them out on three-by-five index cards and stick them around the house, in the car, at work. Say them to yourself over and over. Recite them to the people you live or work with.

As you commit these instructions to memory, perhaps a prayer like the following will help you make the commitment to put memories into action:

Dear God,
I come to you today realizing that I know a lot about minor things and very little about what's truly important. I don't know how to become the disciple you want me to be. Even what little I know I don't put into practice as I should. Forgive me, Lord.

Long ago, your Son spoke the Beatitudes to initiate his followers. Today, I listen to them anew, asking you to initiate me into your ways. Write these words on my heart. Give me an understanding of what these words mean. Most of all, Father, grant me the grace to become the kind of person described here. I believe you when you say:

The poor in spirit are blessed.
Those who mourn will find comfort.
The meek will conquer.
The hungry will be filled.
The merciful will find mercy.
The pure in heart will see you.
The peacemakers will be like you.
The persecuted will receive the kingdom.

Thank you for these transforming words. Let them have their way in my life. Amen.

father... CAN YOU SPARE A DIME?

God only who made us rich can make us poor.

—ELIZABETH B. BROWNING

Scraping the bottom of the barrel. At the end of the rope. Up against the wall. On the rocks. Going under for the third time. One foot in the grave. Down and out. Washed up. Desperate.

These are words and phrases in the vocabulary of failure. You hear them used all the time. You may even use them yourself on occasion. But only at arm's length.

Only half in jest. For defeat is not a language most of us want to speak fluently.

Only failures use such phrases in earnest. Only people who are crawling out of alcoholism or drug addiction or sexual slavery or eating disorders seem able to speak this language comfortably. Go to any support group for recovering addicts and you'll hear the jargon of defeat crop up frequently in their testimonials and confessions.

"I'd inched my way toward destruction."

"I was facing three to five years in prison."

"I was broken by crack."

"My life was quickly falling apart."

"I knew I was losing myself."

"I'd destroyed my career, my marriage, and my children."

Listen to the testimony of

FIRE UP THE BROWSER

Testimonies of Christians in Recovery can be found on the Web at

http://www.christians-in-recovery.com/links/link-test.html

Blessed are the poor in spirit, for theirs is the kingdom of Heaven.[1]

"Reg" and you hear the vocabulary of failure at every turn. "I was lost and undone until I met his Son." Reg was an alcoholic, drinking 2.5 gallons of hard liquor every day. "I'd tried everything, but I couldn't stop drinking."

A pastor friend finally confronted Reg, telling him he'd never recover until he admitted he was unable to help himself. His only hope was to ask God to do for him what he couldn't accomplish on his own.

"I was at a point in my life where I was beaten. We knelt down by a chair in the pastor's office, and he prayed for me. Then I asked God, 'Can I please have some help? I've tried to do this on my own, and I can't stay sober. Please come into my life and help me.'"

Reg has been clean and sober for more than twenty years now. He hasn't had a drink since that day. "Everything I have is his. Without him I would have nothing and be nothing."

If you spend time around Alcoholics Anonymous or Christians in Recovery or any of the other related twelve-step programs, you'll hear people owning up to failure. They do it without embarrassment or vacillation. They look you in the eye and tell you candidly, "I was a mess." Such an admission is the first step required in any twelve-step process: "We admit we are powerless—that our lives have become unmanageable."

In the Beatitudes, Jesus doesn't outline twelve steps—He only has eight. And the Beatitudes aren't directed at alcoholics or drug addicts—they're for disciples. But Jesus begins at the same place recovery programs begin. He asks us to recognize that we're powerless to change our lives by our own efforts. He insists that discipleship can begin only when we have reached the end of ourselves.

LET'S START AT THE VERY BEGINNING

I've been calling the Beatitudes an instruction manual for disciples. And, like most manuals, the Beatitudes have a sequence.

As you put together an appliance or set the digital clock on your new stereo system you need to proceed through specific steps. The same is true when you follow in the footsteps of Jesus. "First do this. Next do that." You begin at step 1, move to step 2, and proceed through to the end. You don't start in the middle of the instructions. ("I think I'll skip the warning about unplugging the garbage disposal, and just go right to the section about putting my hand in. . . ." Ggrrrgghhhhwwwwlllll!)

You can't go to the end and work backward.

There's always a first step to instructions. Get it right, and the foundation is laid for all that follows. Get it wrong, and everything else goes wrong.

As an instruction manual, the Beatitudes are helpful directions for becoming a disciple of Jesus. But a sequence is built into the Beatitudes—an order to their arrangement that must be respected. As you approach the Beatitudes, you can't pick the one you like best and start with it. You can't start in the middle and work outward. As Jesus tells us how to be disciples, he doesn't just tell us *what* to do. He tells us *when* to do it.

Where do you start if you want to follow Jesus? You have to start somewhere. Jesus says you begin with poverty of spirit.

Just between you and me, I wish he'd begun with the "Disciple's Oath." You know the one. It goes like this:

Neither snow nor rain nor heat nor Satan's might will tempt this disciple from the swift completion of my anointed rounds.

That would have been nice. Or failing that, I wish he'd begun with some kind of Spiritual Aptitude Test:

"Do you hate sin? Yes? Very good."

"Do you love God? Hmm. Excellent."

"Do you accept a Trinitarian view of the Godhead and take an amillennial position on the last days?"

"Congratulations! You've passed the first test of discipleship!"

Instead, Jesus begins not with what we think about God or what we think about religion. Jesus begins with what we think about *ourselves*. He cuts through it all and puts his finger on the one spot we'd rather he not touch.

"Tell me who you think you are. Are you here because you consider yourself worthy to be a disciple? Or are you here because being my disciple is your only hope of becoming worthy? When you look in the mirror, are you content with what you see? Or do you despair? Do you have it all together? Or have you discovered how untogether you really are? Careful how you answer, friend. You can't be my disci-

MAIL CARRIER'S CREDO: Neither snow nor rain nor heat nor gloom of night stays these couriers from the swift completion of their appointed rounds.
—U.S. Postal Service

ple until you've seen the truth about yourself."

If Jesus asked you and me to write a classified ad for potential disciples, describing the kind of people who might be qualified for the position, it might sound something like this:

LOOKING FOR A FEW GOOD PEOPLE. *Must be morally sound and biblically literate. Past experience with resisting temptation required. Please submit resume with references. Tax collectors need not apply.*

But the ad Jesus places here in the first Beatitude sounds very different.

WANTED: BREAST-BEATERS. *People who are quick to confess they are sinners. Only those who recognize they are powerless to change themselves need apply. Past failures a must. If you can submit a resume with references, don't bother.*

"Blessed are the poor in spirit, for theirs is the kingdom of heaven." Jesus begins his instructions for discipleship by pronouncing a blessing on those who have discovered destitution of the soul. "Open your eyes," says Jesus. "See yourself as you are. See yourself from a God's-eye view. Know that you're a pauper, a beggar, a spiritual have-not in the kingdom."

Discipleship begins only when we reach the end of ourselves.

TWO PICTURES OF POVERTY

God should have made all men sailors. For it turns out that only drowning men can see him.

—LEONARD COHEN

We meet a variety of poor people in the New Testament—beggars, the blind and the lame, men standing on the street corner hoping someone might offer them a job, people in hopeless debt.

But in all the New Testament, only two individuals are specifically called "poor."

We're introduced to the first one in the gospel of Mark (12:41-42) where we're told of a "poor widow" Jesus sees at the temple. You remember her.

She's the one who put everything she had—"all that she had to live on"—into the collection plate. Her all wasn't much at all. It was only two small copper coins, worth only a fraction of a penny. This widow was poorer than any person I've ever known before she came to the temple—and even poorer after she left.

The second poor person we meet in the New Testament is a beggar called Lazarus (Luke 16:19-21). He's in even worse condition than the widow! He lay at the gate of a rich man, too sick and weak to move. Jesus is graphic in his description of Lazarus's misery: He was "covered with sores" that "the dogs came to lick." Yuck. The only moment of relief for Lazarus came at dinnertime. He hoped that a few crumbs from the rich man's table might be thrown to him.

These poor people had two things in common.[2] The

widow and Lazarus were *destitute*. They had nothing. No resources, no assets, no lines of credit. They lived in abject, unremitting poverty.

And both of them were *dependent*. They couldn't provide for themselves. They were forced to rely on the generosity of others. The widow came to the temple, casting herself on the mercies of God. The beggar sat at the rich man's gate, hoping for a handout.

In our culture, we think being poor means you drive an old car, you can't afford life insurance, and you don't go out to eat very often. But what if being poor means that you have *nothing?* That you're reduced to begging? That your only hope of keeping body and soul together is the generosity of someone else—someone who'll provide for you what you can't provide for yourself?

What if being *spiritually* poor means the same thing?

Could Jesus be saying that discipleship begins only when

we understand just how spiritually destitute, just how God-dependent we really are? That's precisely how one writer understands this Beatitude:

O the bliss of the man who has realized his own utter helplessness, and who has put his whole trust in God, for thus alone can he render to God that perfect obedience which will make him a citizen of the kingdom of heaven![3]

With this Beatitude, Jesus tells us that discipleship can begin only when we picture ourselves as beggars lying sin-sick at the gate of God. We must put ourselves in the widow's place—having nothing of value to offer, having nowhere to turn other than God's mercies. We don't come into the presence of God to offer our strong points and bargain with our "better selves." We come needy and broken, hands outstretched, begging God to provide for us what we have failed (and always will fail) to provide for

ourselves. We're poor, not rich. We're sick, not well. We're sinners, not saints. When that truth comes crashing home for us, says Jesus, then we'll be close to the kingdom of heaven.

A RELUCTANT POVERTY
Poverty is a hateful blessing.
—Vincent of Beauvais

When Jesus says, "Blessed are the poor in spirit," he's telling us something we don't want to hear. Immediately, we're tempted to downgrade this statement from a Beatitude to a platitude. It doesn't really say what it means. It can't mean what it says.

Surely Jesus doesn't mean that the first step of discipleship is a confession of spiritual destitution!

Oh, we'll admit to *some* lack of spiritual resources. We have been overdrawn at the bank of God on occasion. But to say that we're spiritually bank-

rupt, that we haven't so much as two virtues to rub together, that our best is just "filthy rags" in the sight of God—well, that's going too far. We may not be spiritual millionaires, but we're certainly not destitute beggars. C'mon! We fast. We give a tenth of all we get. We go to church every Sunday. Surely Jesus isn't suggesting that the foundational characteristic of a disciple is the willingness to admit, "I'm a wretched sinner."

And dependent too? Is Jesus saying that only those who keep their hand out to God have the right to become disciples?

No sooner does Jesus pronounce a blessing on the "poor in spirit" than our pride wells up, our sense of self boils over, our "Yes, but . . ." spills out. We hate thinking of ourselves as beggars. It's humiliating to recognize that we're qualified to be disciples because we admit poverty, not because we demonstrate

A DEFINITION
plat•i•tude—(noun) [from the French word plat, meaning flat or dull]. 1. the quality or state of being dull or insipid. 2. a banal, trite, or stale remark.
—Webster's Collegiate Dictionary

merit. We'd rather come to Jesus because that's what spiritually rich people do—not because, in our desperation, we have nowhere else to turn.

Of course, sometimes God has to make up for our minor shortfalls—especially at the beginning of our spiritual walk when we're dependent on God's grace and forgiveness. But those times pass, right? In due course, we wean ourselves off God's handouts. We might begin our discipleship as weak dependents, but we grow up to be disciples the old fashioned way—we *earn* it! After all, you can't be constantly begging God to provide for you what you can't provide for yourself. Mature disciples must learn to stand on their own two feet, right?

We hear Jesus talk about spiritual poverty—and we wink at each other. We give that knowing nod. We hope the person sitting next to us is listening closely. "But spiritual poverty is not a necessity for *all* disciples," we tell ourselves. "When Jesus spoke this first Beatitude, he wasn't thinking about me!"

DO YOU HAVE IT OR NOT?

"You say, 'I am rich; I have acquired wealth and do not need a thing.' But you do not realize that you are wretched, pitiful, poor, blind and naked."

—REVELATION 3:17

There are only two kinds of men: the righteous who think they are sinners and the sinners who think they are righteous.

—BLAISE PASCAL

Spiritually speaking, Jesus sees only two kinds of people—the first and the last. There are those who consider themselves rich and those who know themselves to be poor. There are the spiritual haves and the spiritual have-nots.

Which of the two have a better shot at the kingdom of heaven—

according to Jesus?

Do you remember the Pharisee and tax collector in one of Jesus' parables? The Pharisee was rich—he had a pile of good deeds to his credit, a heap of religious and moral trinkets to stack on his side of the scale. He stood in the temple, looked God in the eye, and boasted of his spiritual accomplishments. To borrow Mark Twain's famous phrase, he was a "good man in the worst sense of the word."

The tax collector, on the other hand, couldn't even look up to heaven. He was too bankrupt, too spiritually impoverished to do anything but confess himself a sinner and strike his chest in remorse. Do you remember which of these two men went home justified before God? And do you recall what Jesus said at the end of the story—just in case you missed the point?

MARK TWAIN'S BEST

"When in doubt, tell the truth."

"Clothes make the man. Naked people have little or no influence on society."

"Man is the only animal that blushes—or needs to."

"Always do right—this will gratify some and astonish the rest."

—from the Internet

"For everyone who exalts himself will be humbled,

and he who humbles himself will be exalted."[4]

Or do you recall who Jesus placed at the head of the line when he pictured folks queuing up for the kingdom of heaven? Tax collectors and prostitutes stand in front of Pharisees.[5] Little children are in line ahead of know-it-all adults.[6] One-handed, one-legged, one-eyed people (people who are obviously disabled in some way) come before the healthy and the whole.[7] And camels will fly (or at least pass through the eye of a needle) before a rich man ever gets to the head of the line.[8] Look at the front of the kingdom ranks, and you'll see a lot of ragged clothes, downcast eyes, and outstretched hands. The special place reserved for self-made, self-confident, self-congratulating people is way, way in the back.

Have you considered why Jesus preferred to associate with no-name sinners rather than with the church leaders of his day? Why would he devote himself to those who knew they were sick rather than spend his time with people who considered themselves healthy?[9] Why did Jesus side with the weeping and penitent woman who washed his feet with her hair instead of joining the chorus of condemnation led by Simon the Pharisee?[10] Perhaps because such people can't pretend they are other than what they are—while the rest of us come kicking and screaming to the confession of poverty.

What Jesus tells us about poverty of spirit is obvious, even if it's uncomfortable. Those who are powerless and familiar with failure and just plain needy, those who have nothing—no value to plead, no merit to argue, no rights to claim—are at an advantage in the kingdom of God. They know who they are . . . and who they are not. *Everybody* knows it. It's as obvious as the guilty looks on their faces.

The rest of us (who sometimes imagine God is fortunate to have people like us on his side) are clinging to the spiritual equivalent of fool's gold. We look so righteous on the outside. But inside are sins we won't look at, flaws we hurriedly cover up, failings we would rather deny than confess.

Perhaps it's to people like us that Jesus says: "Better a blatant but self-aware sinner than a covert and self-deceived one. Blessed are the poor in spirit."

The truth is that Jesus doesn't really see only two kinds of people in the world (first and last, rich and poor, haves and have-nots). He sees only *one* kind—spiritual paupers, destitute and dependent on a merciful God.

The only real difference in people is this: Some paupers don't recognize what they are; they spend all their lives preening their filthy rags and proudly savoring their moldy crusts of spiritual bread. But other paupers see themselves clearly, know themselves fully, and run back to their Father who alone has bread to spare.

We all live in spiritual squalor. Some of us just recognize the pigpen our lives have become while others delude themselves into thinking that the pigpen is really a palace.

BLESSED POVERTY

But Satan now is wiser than of yore, and tempts by making rich, not making poor.
—ALEXANDER POPE

How terribly difficult we find it to bow the knee to our God, confess we are starving sinners, and beg for the scraps that fall from his mercy and grace. Yet the bended knee, the bowed head, and the outstretched hand is the posture in which disciples are born.

We always begin discipleship at the end of ourselves.

Until we can make the point-blank declaration that God must do for us what we can't do for ourselves, that our human will has failed, until we admit that we're defeated and utterly destitute before the holiness of our God, we can't even take the first step as disciples. When Jesus says, "Blessed are the poor in spirit," he means, "Only those who have weighed themselves in God's balance and have seen just how wanting they are, have any hope of becoming my disciples."

God can't raise back to life those who refuse to admit they're dead. He can't justify those who don't believe they stand condemned. He can't give the riches of the kingdom to those who proudly deny their need.

So do you want to take the first step of discipleship? Take a good, long, honest look in the mirror. Don't bother viewing yourself through your own self-justifying, self-deceiving eyes. Instead, see yourself through the eyes of a holy God who loves righteousness and hates sin. Admit that left on your own, you are powerless and poor. Recognize your spiritual destitution and absolute dependence on God's mercy. Acknowledge that God loves you in spite of your sinfulness, not because of your sinlessness.

Make a fist. Beat it against your chest. Pray, "God, be merciful to me—a sinner."

Congratulations. If you really meant what you just prayed, you've started down the road to new life. According to Jesus, it's the poor in spirit who will enter the kingdom of heaven. It's those who cry "help" who will be rescued. It's the people who come begging who will win God's approval and receive his assistance. Only spiritual paupers get rich quick in God's kingdom.

We are all desperate, and that is, in fact, the only state appropriate to a human being who wants to know God.
—PHILIP YANCEY[11]

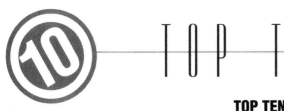

TOP TEN . . . .

TOP TEN SIGNS YOU MAY BE FAKING POVERTY OF SPIRIT

10. Your private prayers are available on CD and cassette.

9. You secretly enjoy patting yourself on the back more than beating yourself on the chest.

8. You often think that most of the world's problems would be solved if people were more like you.

7. You keep a Game Boy in your prayer closet "just in case."

6. You often find yourself mumbling: "Every day in every way, I'm getting better and better."

5. You're considering your own public access cable show, called "Spotlight on Humility."

4. Your wrenching confessions of wrongdoing frequently end with the word "but. . . ."

3. Your "Honk If You Love Jesus" bumper sticker is displayed prominently on your Rolls Royce.

2. You like to sing different words to "Amazing Grace" under your breath:

Amazing grace how sweet the sound

That saved a wretch like you.

How glad I am that I don't sin

Else I might need grace too.

And the **#1** indicator you may be faking poverty of spirit:

Your website address is www.for-such-a-worm-as-i.com

THE STORY OF...

John Newton

A WRETCH LIKE WHO?

Without a doubt, the most popular hymn in America is "Amazing Grace." Catholics, Protestants, and even Unitarians sing this song with feeling. Unfortunately, they don't all sing the same words.

You know the first stanza:

*Amazing grace! How sweet the
   sound!
That saved a wretch like me!
I once was lost, but now am
   found,
Was blind, but now I see.*

That's how most of us remember it. That's the way John Newton wrote it. But it's not the way some hymnals invite us to sing it.

*Amazing grace! How sweet the
   sound!
That saved and strengthened
   me. . . .*

Or, try this on for size:

*Amazing grace! How sweet the
   sound!
That saved and set me free. . . .*

It's that second line modern adapters find so difficult—the one that uses the *W* word. Poets of a former era can be forgiven for excessive language and dramatic flair. It was acceptable to use words like "wretch" when John Newton was writing. But psychologically sensitive, culturally aware, politically correct editors today must find other, less convicting words. People who sing "Amazing Grace" in our churches these days are basically nice people. They're not evil or wicked—at worst, they're dysfunctional. We can't have such people calling themselves "wretches."

But to change this second line to accommodate modern sensibilities destroys the point of the song—and undermines the theology of the man who wrote it.

John Newton knew what he'd been when he used that word. At sea by the age of eleven, he fell into a life that was so wretched, even his crewmates regarded him as little more than an animal. He was a deserter, suffered public floggings, trafficked in human slaves (raping the women and beating the men), and felt no sin was too vile to avoid.[12]

Though dangers and illnesses would sometimes cause him to consider his spiritual condition, Newton's "awakenings" were short-lived and gave way to more wicked exertions. Of this time, Newton said, "I was fast bound in chains. I had little desire and no power at all to recover myself."

Finally, suffering from fever and depression, Newton crept away to a secluded spot and began to pray, "I made no more resolves, but cast myself before the Lord to do with me as he should please."

Two years later, John Newton married his teenage sweetheart and began studying for the ministry. In 1779, he published a hymnal in which 281 of his own works appeared. "Amazing Grace" was one of them. When he chose the word "wretch" to describe himself (and all who sing this song), he did so deliberately. By his own experience (and his theology), Newton knew that only spiritual beggars make good disciples. Only because of wretchedness can grace be so amazing. It does for us what no other power can do.

Christian theology, both Catholic and Protestant, once insisted that what was called a "conviction of sin" was the beginning of conversion. The recognition of one's utter sinfulness was the essential first step toward redemption. . . .[13]

Newton understood this. Those who try to rewrite his song don't. If they do, apparently they're as embarrassed as we are to confess that grace enters our lives only through the door of spiritual poverty.

THINKING IT THROUGH

MONDAY

- We're introduced in this chapter to the only two New Testament characters who are specifically called "poor." Read Mark 12:41-42 and Luke 16:19-31. Describe the condition of the widow and beggar you meet in these passages.
- In what ways do these two people demonstrate *destitution* and *dependency*? What do you see in these verses as evidence of this?
- Have you ever noticed that Jesus has a soft spot for poor, disabled, and rejected people? Think about how often (just in Luke's gospel, for example) Jesus expressed concern for people like this. Read Luke 4:18; 7:22; 11:41; 12:33; 14:13; 18:22; 19:8. Make a list of the ways in which Jesus served these people.

TUESDAY

We haven't a clue what real poverty means—owning nothing but the clothes we stand in, having no food, being forced to sell a daughter into prostitution or a son into slavery. We are wealthy beyond most people's imagining. We consider that a great blessing. But it also may be our greatest curse, for wealth breeds attitudes deadly to the spirit. How does wealth foster the following attitudes? How can these attitudes affect us spiritually? (The list below will give you some clues to think about.)

- Independence
- Pride (1 Timothy 6:17; James 1:10)
- Comfort and complacency (Luke 12:16-21)
- Judging things by the world's standards
- Being tyrannized by the urgent (Matthew 13:22; Luke 6:24-25)
- A temporary rather than eternal perspective (Matthew 19:21-22; 1 Timothy 6:9; James 1:10-11; 5:1-6)

WEDNESDAY

Think about how Jesus was received differently by the rich and the poor:

- Why did so many "rich and famous" people reject Jesus and his message? Consider the rich young ruler (Luke 18:18-25), Simon the Pharisee (Luke 7:36-50), the religious authorities (Matthew 21:42-46), and Herod (Luke 13:31). There were some exceptions to the rule. The centurion (Matthew 8:5-13) was probably middle class. However, he had one flaw—he was a Gentile! And do you remember Zacchaeus (Luke 19:1-9)? He was wealthy, yet still found salvation. Of course, he was also the lowest of the low in another way—he was a tax collector.
- Make a list of the poor people who responded favorably to Jesus. Some of them you can list by name (for example, many of the disciples). Some you will only be able to identify by traits (such as the blind beggar in John 9).
- There are a number of "call" stories in the Gospels—accounts of Jesus inviting

people to become his disciples. The calling of Peter and Matthew are examples of this. There are, however, also a few "failed call" stories—times Jesus invited but was refused. Notice that they usually involve some preoccupation with wealth or material possessions (see Luke 9:57-62; 18:18-25; John 6:25-27,66). What do the following stories tell us about the role wealth plays in turning people away from God? Read Luke 14:16-21; 15:28-32; and Matthew 13:22.

- Is there a central message in all of these stories for those who consider themselves *spiritually* wealthy?

THURSDAY

The passages below contain statements that demonstrate poverty of spirit. Read them aloud. Do these words come easily to your lips? Do they sound natural or peculiar when *you* speak them?

- Ezra 9:5-7
- Job 1:20-21
- Psalm 51:1-17
- Jeremiah 31:19
- Luke 5:8; 15:21; 18:13
- John 3:26-30
- 1 Timothy 1:15-16

FRIDAY

Yesterday, we looked at "words" of poverty. But, sometimes actions speak louder than words. Turn to the gospel of Luke and read the following passages. How—through posture, gesture, facial expression—do these people communicate a sense of their own failure and their need for God? Write down what you observe about them and reflect on whether your own posture before God communicates pride or poverty.

- The man with leprosy (5:12)
- The woman at Simon's house (7:37-38)
- Jairus (8:40-42)
- The crippled woman (13:10-13)
- The tax collector (18:13)

What is the principal lesson you learned this week through your study?

TALKING IT OVER

TEXT: DANIEL 4:28-37

WARM-UP:

We love rags-to-riches stories—ones that celebrate hard work, dedication, and perseverance. The story line can be the same one we've heard a thousand times, but we never tire of it: Poor lad or lass . . . no hopes, no prospects, no supporters . . . a good idea, endless labor, long days . . . setbacks, discouragements, but a never-say-die attitude . . . ultimate success and acclaim.

What are your favorite stories along this line? Can you think of someone whose life mirrors the ghetto-to-boardroom, nobody-to-superstar, pauper-to-prince theme so common to this kind of story? Share with the rest of the group.

Hollywood loves a rags-to-riches story. But the Bible seems partial to another story line. Riches to rags. Remember the prodigal son? He had everything and lost it all. Finally, in the muck of the pigpen he discovered what was important about life. Or how about Moses—from Pharaoh's successor to a shepherd in the wilderness?

Only after forty years of chasing lambs was Moses ready to lead God's people out of Egypt.

One riches-to-rags story, however, powerfully makes the same point as the first Beatitude: the story of Nebuchadnezzar found in Daniel 4:1-37.

1. Have the group leader (or whoever is familiar with the first 27 verses of this chapter) explain Nebuchadnezzar's dream and Daniel's interpretation.
2. Ask one of the group members to read Daniel 4:28-37 out loud.

DISCUSSION:

1. Where do all of Nebuchadnezzar's troubles start? Read one verse in the story that demonstrates the *opposite* of the poverty of spirit.
2. Why was it so important that Nebuchadnezzar "acknowledge the Most High is sovereign" (verse 32)?
3. Describe what happened to Nebuchadnezzar. Does this sound like he suffered from some form of mental illness? What does the mention of sanity

in verse 34 indicate? Did God drive Nebuchadnezzar mad?
4. At the end of this time, Nebuchadnezzar had a different view of God and of himself. Look at verses 34-37. What did he acknowledge about God? What did he confess about himself (or rather *all* people)?
5. Read the last statement in verse 37. Nebuchadnezzar seems to be saying that human pride invites divine humiliation. That was certainly true in his own life. He began rich and proud. He became poor and shamed. He ended up rich again—but humble. Comments?

APPLICATION:

1. Does anybody in the group have a personal riches-to-rags story to share with the group? A time when pride went before a fall?
2. "Human pride invites divine humbling." Do you agree with that statement? If so, why do we prefer to congratulate ourselves rather than confess? Aren't we just setting ourselves up for a fall?

3. Chances are you'll have opportunity this week to say those dreaded words, "I was wrong." How easy is it for you to admit error? Isn't a willingness to confess wrong at the heart of being "poor in spirit"? Why do we find it so difficult?

4. Poverty of spirit doesn't come naturally to us. Sometimes it seems that the only way we get over pride and self-satisfaction is to have it beaten out of us—like Nebuchadnezzar. What are some ways God is working in your life to help you "acknowledge that the Most High is sovereign"?

5. On a spiritual poverty scale of 1 to 10 (1 = "I think just like the Pharisee—Thank God I'm not like other people"; 10 = "I think just like the tax collector—Be merciful to me a sinner") where would you place yourself? Where would your spouse or closest friend put you? Where would most people who know you well put you on this scale?

COOL DOWN:

Think about this statement: "We only begin discipleship at the end of ourselves." If poverty of spirit is the first step of becoming a disciple, indicate to the group how far along you are. Be careful. Don't start boasting about your humility or you'll have to read this chapter again!

The "Living It Out" section includes a prayer. Pray this together as a group.

LIVING IT OUT

Several of the twelve steps in many recovery programs mirror the lessons of the first Beatitude. The first step, "We admit we are powerless—that our lives have become unmanageable," is followed by a fourth, "We have made a searching moral inventory of ourselves," and a fifth, "We have admitted to God, to ourselves, and to another human being the exact nature of our wrongs." Those three steps comprise a useful and practical approach to poverty of spirit.

Have you admitted to yourself that you are powerless? Do you admit that your life has become unmanageable? If you need convincing of that fact, it helps to take a "searching moral inventory." Don't review every sin, every failing, every flaw. Just write down the *recurring* problems—the sins you recognize, repent of, and then commit all over again. Everyone has failings that no amount of self-control and discipline will conquer. Is it anger? Lust? Greed? Impatience? Gluttony? Selfishness? Pride? Write them down. Cover a page with the evidence of your own helplessness.

The more honest, the more "searching" this inventory, the more convicted you'll be that your life has become unmanageable. And if you are not convinced now—looking at that sheet of paper before you—just wait a while. Sooner or later, now or in the future, you'll come to the end of yourself and confess that you can't make it on your own.

Once we admit to ourselves our own poverty—our spiritual destitution—the time has come to admit it to God. Perhaps a prayer like the following would help you give voice to what you have seen in yourself:

Dear God,
Be merciful to me, a sinner. I look at myself and feel ashamed. I have no merit, no goodness to boast of. I've tried to run my own life, direct my own ways, and I've failed miserably. I repeatedly fall short and embarrass myself. I live so far below what you want of me.

Father, if I'm to be your disciple, it will happen only because of the mercy you give me. I'm dependent on you for my very breath— how much more for the power to become your faithful follower. Into the vacuum of my life, pour your power and will. Grant me the spiritual resources to become the person you want me to be. Give me the scraps from your table and I'll be satisfied. And teach me to remember where my spiritual sustenance comes from—always from you. Amen.

Ah, but we're not finished yet. Now comes the part about admitting your poverty to someone else. Telling yourself the truth about yourself is good—but how soon we forget! And telling God the truth about yourself is great—but he already knows, doesn't he? Telling another human being (someone you know, someone you have to see at church or work)—now that's hard. It means there's at least one person in this world that you're not fooling (someone who hears you at your poorest and loves you anyway). So find someone you can trust and show your "searching moral inventory" to him or her. Go over it item by item. Make no excuses. Offer no justifications. Don't gloss over the ugliness of it all. Be poor, for once in your life, and experience that attribute which Jesus insists is the first step toward the kingdom of heaven.

IN A WORD

Poverty of spirit is the capacity to say, **"I was wrong"**—and mean it. That simple sentence may be the most difficult one you'll ever speak on a consistent, daily basis. Saying it quickly and sincerely is the essence of the sort of spirit which Jesus calls "poor."

Come MOURN WITH US

What soap is for the body tears are for the soul.

—JEWISH PROVERB

The two of them walked into my office and sat down. Before either of them said a word, I knew their story. I'd heard it many times before.

She'd been unfaithful. He was devastated.

The affair had gone on for months. He discovered what was happening, yet still the affair continued.

They separated. She hadn't been able to see the children. The family was going down the drain financially. But she wouldn't give up her lover.

They sat there and talked to me about the struggles they'd endured over the years. They acknowledged the agony they were enduring at the moment. They calmly discussed whether the marriage could be healed.

I asked her gently, "Do you know what you're doing is wrong?" I thought perhaps she'd gone temporarily insane, that maybe she'd lost connection with everything she claimed to believe.

"Oh yes." She looked me straight in the eye. "I know this is wrong. It's a sin against my husband, against my children, and against God. I never thought I'd be capable of such a thing. What I've done is evil."

"What I haven't heard you say," I told her, "is that you *regret* what you've done, that you're heartbroken over it, that you repent of this and are willing to put a stop to it."

> **ADULTERY**
> About 21 percent of men and 13 percent of women admit to having had sex with someone other than their spouse. The most likely to stray? Nearly one third of men 45-60 years of age have extramarital affairs.
>
> —National Opinion Research Center

Blessed are those who mourn, for they will be comforted.[1]

You would think I'd slapped her. Her back straightened. Her anger flashed. She tossed her head. "I don't regret it. I know it's wrong, but I don't care!"

Did you know it's quite possible to confess yourself a sinner—and be dry-eyed as you do so? Did you realize that you can see yourself in all your spiritual poverty—but feel no crippling grief or rending remorse? Have you understood yet that there is all the difference in the world between recognizing what a sinner you are and weeping over the fact?

HARD WORDS

What in the world was Jesus thinking when he said that the second characteristic of a true disciple is the capacity to mourn?

The business of becoming his follower would be so much more attractive if Jesus had spoken of, say, inner peace: "Blessed are those who accept themselves. Blessed are those who develop healthy self-esteem." Now that's

the sort of Beatitude we want to hear. But *mourning?* How does Jesus expect to win friends and influence people with ideas like that? What kind of recruitment slogan can you make out of sorrow? "Come weep with us!" Oh, that'll pack 'em in!

Jesus has already said that disciples need to be "poor in spirit." But now it sounds like disciples must be depressed as well as destitute.

Mourning: Properly and primarily to lament for the dead; then any other passionate lamenting . . . to grieve with a grief which so takes possession of the whole being that it cannot be hid.[2]

Mourn. This isn't a soft word Jesus uses here to define a disciple. He isn't speaking of an occasional sniffling or getting the blues once in a great while. He's referring to what the

mothers were doing when King Herod killed their babies.[3] It's what Mary and Martha were doing when they visited the tomb of their recently buried brother Lazarus.[4] This is what the disciples were doing after Jesus was crucified.[5] Blessed are those who have been cut to the very core of their being. Blessed are those who are beside themselves with grief. Blessed are those who cry and wail and weep uncontrollably!

Sounds fun. Where do I sign up?

If Jesus had asked me to put together the directions for becoming his disciples, I don't think I would have included mourning. Who could have guessed that God wants people who weep? Who would have thought that genuine discipleship is the hard-born child of tears? Yet Jesus insists only those who experience a deep and painful sense of loss, only those who have known a death that must be mourned

THE FIVE STAGES OF GRIEF
1. Denial
2. Anger
3. Bargaining
4. Depression
5. Acceptance

can become his true disciples.

The one thing harder than hearing this word about mourning is hearing what Jesus wants us to cry about. He pronounces a blessing on tears—but not just *any* tears. He says that weeping is good—but not just *any* weeping. There are all kinds of grief in this life. But it's a special kind of grief that Jesus blesses and names as necessary for those who want to be his disciples.

How do I know? Remember that the Beatitudes are Christ's instruction manual on discipleship. There's a *sequence* to the steps we are asked to take. These are not eight "unrelated but useful skills" for following Jesus. Each Beatitude lays a foundation for the ones to follow. Later steps depend on those that come before. You can't isolate one Beatitude and then pour into it any meaning you want. Each Beatitude is defined by the ones that precede it.

WHAT'S IN A TEAR?

Tears are mostly water and salt. However, tears resulting from sadness, anger, fear, or joy vary chemically from those caused by smelling onions. Emotional tears may be nature's method of removing chemicals built up by stress from the body.

—Psychiatry Research Laboratories

If you want to understand mourning, you must see it through the lens of poverty of spirit. The kind of mourning Jesus blesses in the second Beatitude is rooted in the poverty of spirit he blessed in the first. It takes disciples who have faced their own destitution before God to engage in the kind of weeping Jesus recommends. Only those who have reached the end of themselves really know what to cry about.

That's the hardest part. Jesus isn't recommending a free-floating depression. He's being very specific. He expects us to lament *ourselves*. Having seen who we are before God, we are called to mourn what we see. It isn't enough to recognize ourselves as sinners— we must grieve over that condition.

You might think that facing up to your spiritual poverty would automatically move you to tears. But don't kid yourself!

It's entirely possible to know you're a wretch—and be quite content with the fact. With this second Beatitude, Jesus drags us from navel-gazing about sinfulness to a lament that motivates us to do something.

AN ABSENCE OF MOURNING

I wept not, so to stone within I grew.

—Dante

King David lusted after Bathsheba. He slept with her even though she didn't belong to him. Then he killed her husband to cover up what he'd done. Finally, he brought her into his palace to become his wife.

Do you know the story of David and Bathsheba? (Read 2 Samuel 11–12 if you've forgotten the details.) You may recall Nathan's confrontation of David's sin and the sad story of the poor man with one little lamb. You might have read David's response to Nathan's rebuke—"I

THE KING IS DEAD?

Which of these countries still have some form of monarchy—Britain, the Netherlands, Norway, Sweden, Denmark, Belgium, Jordan, or Saudi Arabia?

Answer:
All of the above

have sinned against the LORD" (2 Samuel 12:13).

For the most part, most of us have entirely missed the moral of this story.

The lesson we usually take from David's failure is that even a good man like David can forget himself and forget what sin is. Maybe David went temporarily insane, and he just couldn't tell the difference between right and wrong. The solution (in our understanding) is for David to admit he has sinned. Nathan's role is to help David come to that insight and develop a little poverty of spirit.

But David's difficulty was not what he *knew* about sin. It was what he *felt* about sin— or, rather, what he *failed* to feel. David certainly knew he'd done wrong, he just didn't hurt over what he had done. He knew how to confess his sins, but he'd forgotten how to weep over them.

Remember that the events of this story took many months to unfold. Enough time elapsed between David's

fornication and Nathan's confrontation for Bathsheba to discover she is pregnant, for David to have her husband killed, and for the child of that union to be born. We're talking at least nine months from the evening David goes walking on his roof to the day that Nathan walks into the throne room. Maybe even a year or more.

During that long interval, do you think David was unaware that he had sinned? Had he conveniently forgotten what Moses said about adultery and murder? Hardly. All through this time—every Sabbath—David went to the temple knowing there was blood on his hands. Each Sabbath he offered sacrifices, asking God to forgive his sins. Each Sabbath, he bowed before God and confessed himself a sinner—"Lord, I lost my temper this week; I drank too much the other night; and, oh yes, there is that matter of Uriah and Bathsheba. Forgive

ADULTERY: IMMORAL OR ILLEGAL?

Thirty-five percent of Americans believe that adultery should be a crime. It's illegal in twenty-eight states, and a felony in five.

—Gallup Poll

me, Lord, for I have sinned."

David knew he sinned long before Nathan arrived. He understood that adultery and murder are wrong. But he didn't take his sin seriously. He rationalized and excused and justified himself to the point that he didn't feel all that bad about what he had done. David learned to do something you and I do all the time—he practiced confession of sin without the unpleasantry of hot, bitter tears.

Until Nathan told his story. Until the guilt crowded and crushed. Until David began to feel his sin where it hurt.

You do not delight in sacrifice,
    or I would bring it;
you do not take pleasure in
    burnt offerings.
The sacrifices of God are a
    broken spirit;
a broken and contrite heart,
O God, you will not despise.[6]

Nathan came not to educate David about wrongdoing,

but to *wound* him with his wrongdoing. David needed to do more than see himself as a sinner, he needed to bleed over his sin and the separation it caused with his God. What Nathan released in David was not a sudden awareness of sin but a torrent of tears. For the first time, David felt what he had done and was driven to weep.

POVERTY WITHOUT MOURNING

He who confesses his sin and does not turn away from it is like one bathing and holding on to a defiling reptile.

—ADDA BEN AHABA

What is mourning? It's the realization that failure and sin and guilt can only be addressed by treating them with the seriousness they deserve. Mourning is bitter tears, a broken heart, a burning shame, a cutting guilt. It's weeping, wailing, and grieving. It's sorrow to the point of exhaustion, remorse to the edge of despair. Mourning is a killing pain that demands the death either of the sinner or the sin.

It is one of the greatest needs among God's people today.

But the sad truth is this: *We don't want to mourn.* As hard as we find it to admit poverty of spirit, we would rather stick with poverty than move on to mourning. Okay, we'll confess we are sinners. We'll admit to spiritual bankruptcy. Just don't make us lament who we are. Mourning might mean we have to change.

It's easy to grow comfortable with poverty of spirit. We learn to admit without embarrassment that we have no merit or distinction. We wallow— and even glory—in our utter dependency on the mercies of God. We boldly wear "bankrupt" signs around our necks and expectantly hold out our hands for God's forgiveness. We tell ourselves that poverty of spirit is enough.

And that's the problem. Having learned to see our sin clearly, many of us never move on to taking sin seriously. Drowning in an ocean of cheap grace, it's difficult for us to understand just how ugly and hurtful our "little failings" can be. What are a few sins compared to "so great a salvation"? Sin loses its gravity—and we lose an incentive for doing something to rid ourselves of it.

Poverty of spirit—detached from mourning—is confession of sin without remorse. It's admitting failure with no sense of shame attached. It's learning to say "I was wrong" without having to say "I'm sorry." It treats sin as a hard fact of life, but doesn't permit much anguish over it. It allows that into every life some sin will fall, but then erects an umbrella against guilt.

Poverty without mourning is the prodigal son coming to himself in the pigpen—but

BANKRUPTCY
More than one million families file for bankruptcy each year in the United States. The average family to do so has an annual income of $20,500, credit card debt of $20,700, and a total debt of $51,000.
—American Bankruptcy Institute

MOURNING IS HARD WORK
It takes only seventeen facial muscles to smile, but forty-three muscles to form a frown.
—The Book of Answers

deciding to stay and wallow for a while longer. It's the tax collector beating his breast—and then shrugging and going back to his old way of life. It's David offering sacrifices instead of a broken and contrite heart. It's the woman who says, "I know it's wrong, but I don't regret it."

That's why mourning follows poverty of spirit in the Beatitudes. Having said he wants disciples who know how to confess, Jesus goes on to say he needs disciples who know how to blush.

WE ARE MISSING MOURNING

Repentance is pain, accompanied by the idea of oneself as cause.

—SPINOZA

We've been conditioned by our culture to see guilt and shame as evil things, to be avoided when possible and psychoanalyzed when not. The only thing worse than doing wrong is feeling guilty about it.

If you don't believe me, ask your therapist.

It's tempting for us, then, to position religion as the great escape from the evil of guilt. We all but promise that if people come to Jesus, they need never feel the pangs of remorse again. The Bible is cheapened into a resource book for soothing shamed consciences. And the church is reduced to dispensing easy forgiveness and positive thoughts.

What do we do, then, with this second Beatitude? Jesus insists that true disciples know how to mourn over their sins. They're confident enough of God that they can afford to be ashamed of themselves. They can grieve and lament over what they have done and who they have become.

If we're a bit afraid of guilt, how do we deal with such a hard and confrontive teaching? We resist it.

Oh, we can mourn over *everyone else's* sins. We read the paper and grieve over the deplorable state of our nation.

The tears roll down our cheeks as we talk about other people's abortions or sexual orientations or ethical standards. We lament how much sin there is these days, even in the church.

And we imagine that we demonstrate discipleship by how disturbed we get over the sins of those around us—when, in fact, this Beatitude insists discipleship is demonstrated best when we are disturbed about our own sin!

But we find it difficult to work up a good grief for *personal wickedness*. We've replaced the great lament with an occasional "Oops!" We've substituted a knowing wink and a dismissive shrug for the "broken and contrite heart." We sin, we pause momentarily, we confess, and then we bound back to the rush of our lives as if nothing really happened. Indeed, for too many of us, nothing of significance did. Oops. Wink. Shrug.

And if we find it difficult to take mourning personally, we find it nearly impossible to make mourning a way of life.

We've learned to limit weeping to the initial stages of discipleship. Like hazing, mourning is a distasteful experience followers of Jesus must endure before they can become full-fledged disciples and move on to the real business of the kingdom. Repeated, profound, continual mourning is, for us, an obvious sign of spiritual weakness. Spiritual maturity is a matter of getting past mourning and getting on with more important matters.

We imagine that real disciples quickly clear their plates of mourning to make room for the "meat and potatoes" of Christianity—when, in fact, this Beatitude insists discipleship is really a matter of making mourning our daily bread!

There is no greater business, no more important matter, than the willingness of disciples to see their sins and feel grief over them. Mourning doesn't go away. You don't get weeping out of your system. Repentance isn't a temporary condition we recover from and move on. Godly sorrow is a characteristic of life lived in the shadow of the cross that won't be eclipsed or sent packing. There's no "cure" for mourning—except, maybe, complacency with sin.

GOOD NEWS FOR THOSE WHO MOURN

Sorrow, my friend, I owe my soul to you.
—MOTHER M. ALPHONSA

Why are we so afraid to mourn? Is it because the experience of guilt is so unpleasant? Do we suspect that the first sign of mourning might trigger an avalanche of remorse that could sweep us away? Is our experience of grace so limited that we fear grieving a sin God cannot forgive?

I think about that woman who would rather sin than mourn. Only in tears will she find the path to healing. I think about David and his awful sin. A broken heart was the needed remedy on his way back to God. I think about you and me. What have we to fear from tears? In mourning is the seed of joy, the cradle of comfort, and the beginning of the road to recovery.

"Blessed are those who mourn, for they will be comforted."

Do you notice the verbs in this statement? "Mourn" and "will be comforted." They're active and then passive, something we do and something done to us. There's an implied contract in this Beatitude. When we attend to the mourning, God will take care of the comfort. Our business is to grieve, God's business is to console. We humble ourselves, God raises us up. We weep, God wipes away our tears. When we do our part, Jesus promises that the God of all comfort will do his.

How strange! All along, we've tried to comfort ourselves. All along, we've expected our parents or our spouses or the church to make it stop hurting. We've fled from mourning, avoided remorse like the plague, run whenever guilt reared its ugly head. We've taken refuge in the sort of painless forgiveness that sinners are quick to bestow on themselves. We don't want to mourn. We're afraid to weep.

But in our headlong flight, we run smack into the brick wall of this second Beatitude.

And, to our surprise, we discover that when we mourn, we receive God's comfort. When we let ourselves be crushed by the weight of sin, we find a God who lifts all burdens. And when we permit grief to undo us, we experience a relief only God affords.

This is my last message to you: in sorrow seek happiness.
—DOSTOYEVSKY

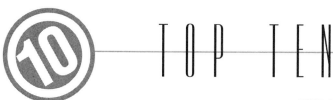 T O P   T E N . . .

TOP TEN STUPID PENANCE TRICKS

10. You sign up for a full year of church nursery duty—and you don't even have kids.

9. You feel so guilty about your past that you spend long hours pouring over books like this one!

8. You declare a fast to the death—but only from hominy, succotash, and brussels sprouts.

7. You dramatically increase your sacrificial giving by putting double coupons in the collection plate.

6. Whenever you see a gas station with a sign reading, "Clean Restrooms," you do.

5. You take Paul's "buffeting your body" to mean compulsory attendance at any and every buffet.

4. You commit to wearing only plaids and polyester.

3. You punish yourself for sins by watching endless reruns of "The Brady Bunch."

2. You adopt that old country ditty, "I've got tears in my ears from lying on my back in my bed while I cry over you," as your spiritual theme song.

And the **#1** stupid penance trick:

Laxatives.

THE STORY OF . . .

George Wallace

THE POLITICS OF RAGE

The life of George C. Wallace sounds like something from Paul Harvey's "The Rest of the Story." It comes in two parts: the sad, earlier life and the hard but hopeful remainder. Even more dramatic is a tragic event in the middle that brought life-changing consequences for the man from Alabama.

In 1962, Wallace ran for governor on a platform that was blatantly racist. He promised to fight integration to the point of defying federal orders and personally blockading schoolhouse doors. He ended his inaugural address with the infamous statement, "I say segregation now, segregation tomorrow, segregation forever." That summer, he refused to allow black students to register at the University of Alabama until forced to do so by the threat of military intervention. Through his tenure as governor and a run for the presidency in 1968, Wallace spouted racial hatred while blacks were beaten and jailed, black churches were burned, and black children were murdered.

Elected governor a second time in 1970, Wallace began to signal a shift in his racial stance. Perhaps he had grown weary of building his political aspirations on other people's fears and prejudices. Or perhaps (as a good politician) he was merely sensing a change in the cultural wind. But, by the time he ran for the presidency in 1972, his message had become more populist and less bigoted.

Then came May 15, 1972—and the rest of the story. While campaigning in Laurel, Maryland, Wallace was shot five times, leaving him paralyzed and in constant pain. Two years later—confined to a wheel chair, divorced from his second wife, without use of his legs, and lacking control of bodily functions—Wallace was a broken, pathetic figure. He was a man who finally understood the meaning of suffering. He was a man who had come to realize what suffering he had caused others.

While being driven home one evening, he passed the open doors of the Dexter Avenue Baptist Church, a black congregation, where years earlier Martin Luther King, Jr., had stood in the pulpit and denounced Wallace for his treatment of African-Americans. Overcome with remorse, Wallace stopped the car, was helped into his wheelchair, and wheeled up the aisle to the stunned surprise of the assembly. There, Wallace tearfully confessed he had been wrong, apologized for the suffering he had caused, and asked the blacks of Alabama to forgive him.

It was an expression of remorse he was to repeat on numerous occasions in the following years—publicly, before black audiences on campuses and at conventions, and privately, to black leaders like Coretta Scott King and Jesse Jackson. During two more terms as governor (1974 and 1982), he built bridges to the black community, developed relationships with prominent black leaders, and worked to undo some of the damage his own racist rhetoric had caused.

Until the very end, while bedridden and deaf, he still received visits from friends, both black and white, and met with groups of both races for prayer.

Not all blacks forgave Wallace. The damage he did and the pain he caused was great. But the story of George Wallace is not about forgiveness, but about penance. Here is a man who was tragically flawed and terribly wrong. It took five bullets and horrific suffering to bring him to his knees. But once broken, he had the courage to face his hatred and prejudice, repent, confess, and then spend the remainder of his life attempting to atone and make restitution.

In 1997, the Turner Network made a docudrama on the life of George Wallace, starring Gary Sinise. Brilliantly written and acted, it captures the career and struggles of Wallace in a powerful way. (For more information, go to www.tnt.turner.com/movies/tntoriginals/wallace/) You might want to check it out at your local video store. It is a moving portrait of hatred, suffering, transformation, and hope. Most of all, it is a story about mourning.

THINKING IT THROUGH

MONDAY

Some people think discipleship is backward to common sense and popular wisdom. This inversion of normal thinking is common for Jesus. Do the following exercises with this idea in mind.

- Jesus makes a number of "success" statements that contradict our normal rules for getting ahead in life. Write out the following statements and, beside each one, write out the world's contrasting version of success.

1. "Love your enemies, do good to them, and lend to them without expecting to get anything back. Then your reward will be great" (Luke 6:35).
2. "Go, sell everything you have and give to the poor, and you will have treasure in heaven" (Mark 10:21).
3. "For whoever exalts himself will be humbled, and whoever humbles himself will be exalted" (Matthew 23:12).
4. "So do not worry, saying, 'What shall we eat?' or 'What shall we drink?' or 'What shall we wear?' . . . But seek first his kingdom and his righteousness, and all these things will be given to you as well" (Matthew 6:31,33).

- Nowhere are the paradoxes of the kingdom more evident than in the Beatitudes. How do the following Beatitudes confront conventional wisdom? (Write down your answers. It will help you to think carefully.) The poor are well off, the sad are happy, the meek are mighty, the hungry are full, the rejected are accepted.

TUESDAY

None of the Beatitudes is quite as contrary to our sense of the way life works than "Blessed are those who mourn." Read the following passages where the word "mourn" occurs and write out a definition of the word based on the context in which it is used.

- Nehemiah 1:3-4
- Psalm 38:1-11; 42:8-11
- Lamentation 5:1-22
- Matthew 2:16-18
- Mark 16:9-10
- Luke 23:27-30
- James 4:8-10
- Revelation 21:3-4

WEDNESDAY

"There is a time for everything . . . a time to weep and a time to laugh, a time to mourn and a time to dance" (Ecclesiastes 3:1,4). Christianity doesn't call us to a life of unremitting tears. It's not, in the end, a religion for ascetics. But it does teach that *when* you choose to laugh or cry, *what* you weep or rejoice over is important. Notice the following passages—some of them recommending joy (or laughter) and some sorrow. Why is one thing commended in some verses and condemned in others?

- Joy is approved—Psalm 126:2-3; Matthew 5:11-12; Luke 15:4-7; Acts 5:41; 8:39; Romans 12:15; Galatians 5:22; Philippians 4:4; 1 Thessalonians 5:16
- Joy is discouraged—Job 20:5; Proverbs 14:13; Ecclesiastes 2:1-2; Luke 6:25; James 4:9
- Mourning is approved— Nehemiah 1:4; Job 5:11; Psalms 126:5-6; Ecclesiastes 7:3-4; Jeremiah 6:26; 25:34; Joel 2:12-13; John 16:20; Romans 12:15; James 4:9; 5:1
- Mourning is discouraged— Nehemiah 8:9-10; Malachi 2:13-14; Matthew 9:14-15; Luke 8:52; 23:27-28

THURSDAY

We studied David as an example of someone who sinned but didn't take his sin seriously. Reread the story of David and Bathsheba (2 Samuel 11–12). The Bible contains other examples of people who wouldn't mourn over their sins. Read the following stories and comment on (1) how each main character demonstrates a lack of mourning, and (2) how a willingness to mourn might have changed the story.

- Genesis 4:9—The case of the murderous brother
- 2 Samuel 13:1-17—The case of the lustful brother
- Deuteronomy 17:14-17; 1 Kings 10:14-11:6—The case of the greedy king
- Hosea 2:2-13—The case of the unfaithful wife
- 2 Corinthians 5:1-2—The case of the immoral Christian and his equally immoral church

FRIDAY

When Jesus says that disciples should "hunger and thirst for righteousness," no one thinks of this as a temporary condition. We understand most of the Beatitudes as enduring character traits that become constants in the lives of disciples. For most of us, though, this ongoing quality disturbs us when it comes to the first two Beatitudes. We want poverty of spirit and mourning to be our *initiation* into discipleship—painful, but short-lived. We certainly don't want to adopt these traits as permanent and necessary attributes.

- Read this brief history of Peter and notice the recurring themes of mistake, rebuke, and repentance: Matthew 4:18-20; 14:25-31; 16:15-23; 18:21-22; 26:33-35, 69-75; Luke 5:4-8; John 13:5-9; 18:10-11; Acts 10:9-16; Galatians 2:11-14.
- Did Peter ever get over the need to recognize and repent of his sinful ways? Was there ever a point in his life when he became too mature—too advanced in his faith—to bother with poverty of spirit and mourning?

TALKING IT OVER

TEXT:
MATTHEW 26:69–27:26

WARM-UP:
Read "The Politics of Rage—The Story of George Wallace" beginning on page 62.

All of us have regrets—words we'd like to take back, reactions we wish we could undo, sins we'd love to erase. There are three basic ways to deal with regrets: we can deny them, we can wallow in them, or we can repent of them. The story you just read hints at each of these approaches.

1. George Wallace could have denied any responsibility (and hence guilt) for the suffering endured by blacks in Alabama. What could he have told himself to take himself off the hook? How do excuses, rationalizations, and minimalizations (all good psychological techniques for handling guilt) keep us from *feeling* what we have done?

2. Wallace could have (and probably did) spend a lot of time wallowing in guilt. Would it have been easy for him to get stuck in his wallowing? Do you think mourning could have killed him?

3. The story ends with Wallace repenting and grieving over his wrongs. What do you imagine he felt that night in front of the Dexter Avenue Baptist Church? What do you think the people in the pews were feeling?

DISCUSSION:
There are three characters in the story of the crucifixion of Jesus who illustrate each of these approaches to dealing with guilt.

1. Read Matthew 27:11-26.
- Did Pilate believe Jesus was innocent of the charges against him?
- Did he have the power to release Jesus?
- What was it that finally made Pilate's decision to have Jesus killed?
- What symbolic act did Pilate use to shift blame for Jesus' death?
- Did this act actually absolve him of guilt or was it merely a technique to minimize or rationalize his own role?
- We know Pilate's wife lost sleep over his role in Jesus' execution. Do you think Pilate ever lost any sleep about what he had done that day? Why, or why not?

2. Read Matthew 27:1-5.
- Matthew tells us that Judas was "seized with remorse." What does that mean? What caused his remorse? What did his remorse lead him to do initially?
- What did Judas hope to accomplish by taking the money back to the chief priests and elders? Did he think they would release Jesus because he felt bad about what he'd done?
- Judas was remorseful. But was he *repentant?* It's one thing to stand before the chief priests and say, "I have sinned," trying to undo the consequences of his betrayal. It's another thing to stand before God and say, "I have sinned," asking to be forgiven of betrayal. Do you think Judas was willing to do the latter? Why, or why not?

3. Read Matthew 26:69-75.
- The Bible doesn't tell us that Peter was "seized with remorse"—only that he "remembered" and "wept bitterly." Did Peter feel as much sorrow for what he had done as Judas did? Less? More?

- In God's eyes, was Peter's denial any less horrible than the betrayal of Judas? Were both sins equally atrocious?
- Judas "went out" and hanged himself. Peter "went out" and wept bitterly. What was the difference between these two responses to regret?
- How do you imagine Peter felt the first time he talked to the risen Christ? Embarrassed? Ashamed? Insecure? Broken? What does his willingness to endure these emotions (as opposed to Judas, who couldn't bear to face the consequences of what he had done) say about Peter, his heart, and his repentance?

APPLICATION:

1. Does anyone in the group have a story about dealing with regrets that parallels Pilate's denial, Judas's wallowing, or Peter's repentance?
2. What's the essential difference between moaning and mourning? Which are you more likely to do when confronted with sin?

3. In the previous chapter, we talked about the need to confess, "I was wrong." In this chapter, we learned that mourning is a matter of coupling confession of wrong with a willingness to repent and say, "I am truly sorry." Is there someone you would like to say "I'm sorry" to? Can you name that person to the group and confess why an apology is necessary? This week, a letter or phone call of apology to that person might be appropriate.

COOL DOWN:

What's your reaction to this material on mourning?

_____ I don't get what all the fuss is about.
_____ There are a few people in this group who really need to hear this!
_____ This cuts too close to the bone to be comfortable.
_____ I love to mourn because I love to feel God's comfort.
_____ Other:

The prayer in the "Living It Out" section speaks to God of our desire to become mourners. Pray this together as a group as you close your time.

LIVING IT OUT

"Penance" has a bad name among some Christians. In certain traditions, this sacrament conjures up notions of "earning your way to heaven" and "atoning for sin by your own efforts." Yet is there a spiritual truth in the idea of penance that our evangelical tradition has lost?

Some religious groups affirm penance as a tool that helps people take sin seriously. It's a way of making repentance practical. While we're often content to leave repentance relatively undefined ("Uh, I guess it means to turn from sin"), other traditions speak very explicitly of three matters involved in true penance.

Use penance language in thinking about a specific sin of your own. Do you have some sin, some nagging habit or vice that you haven't taken as seriously as you should? You know it's wrong. You know God disapproves. But you can't seem to muster up much mourning. You keep playing with it. Write that sin down here:

_____
(My Sin:)

The first step taken by the penitent must be *contrition* —a state in which one *sorrows* for sin, *detests* sin, and *resolves* not to commit that sin again. Interestingly, some traditions teach that this is a supernatural condition— that we cannot make ourselves mourn over and turn from sin— that only the Spirit of God can produce true contrition.

So why not ask God to help you sorrow for sin? Why not pray for contrition? You may want to use the following prayer to ask God to help you mourn.

Father,
I am a sinner. I know it. But I have lived so long in sin, there are times when I don't feel my sin or grieve for my sin as I should. Please forgive me for that. Make me more sensitive to sin. Stab my dead heart awake and cause me to mourn my transgressions. Teach me to hate my sin and turn from it. Bless me with the gift of brokenness and tears. Let me mourn in your presence, so that, in your presence, I can find the comfort I need and the courage to live better. Amen.

Second, you must *confess.* Of course, most of us don't mind confession as long as it's limited to vague, generic, clichéd expressions. But what about the idea that confession should be specific and detailed, that each and every sin should be named rather than resorting to mumbled euphemisms? It's embarrassing for confession to get so specific.

Take the sin you listed above. There is someone to whom you should confess yourself, naming *specific* sin, stating *in detail* your remorse, and indicating the *particulars* of your determination to do better. Perhaps it's a spouse, a child, a coworker. Perhaps this confession should be directed toward God. But you and I could stand a little more specificity when it comes to confession.

Finally, penance involves *satis-faction*—the acceptance of a penalty designed primarily to drive home the realization that sin costs. Sometimes, satisfaction can take the form of *restitution* (as when you give back stolen goods). But most of the time, satisfaction is *vicarious*—Jesus paid for our sins, but we identify with his suffering by enduring a little suffering of our own. Fasting, a period of silence, a monetary gift to the needy—there are many ways to put your actions where your tears are.

Frankly, I like the tradition of penance. I appreciate the way those who practice it have struggled to think more deeply about repentance and to make mourning practical. Contrition, confession, and satisfaction—makes a pretty good three-point sermon on mourning.[7]

IN A WORD

Mourning is the willingness to say, **"I'm sorry."** Having seen our sin, this Beatitude teaches us to *feel* our sin and find the courage to do better. It marries heartfelt contrition with an earnest desire to change.

The MIGHTY MEEK

Thirty years of our Lord's life are hidden in these words of the gospel: "He was subject unto them...."

—JACQUES BÉNIGNE BOSSUET

have a dog named Shenzii (after one of the hyenas in *The Lion King*). Actually, my daughter, Sarah, has a dog named Shenzii (the name was her idea—so was the dog). She' a pretty thing. (The dog, not my daughter. Well, my daughter is pretty too. Actually, she's quite beautiful.) Half Labrador and half Husky, big and strong, smart as a doorknob (again, I mean the dog).

Sarah and I took Shenzii through obedience school. Every Thursday night for two months we gathered with other proud owners of "man's best friend." We learned "Sit" and "Stay" and "Come." We worked on "Heel" and "Fetch" and "Speak." And then we started training the dogs.

Shenzii was the star student of her class. She learned all that we asked. We spoke, she responded. We commanded, she obeyed. (I won-

dered if I could use the same techniques on Sarah.) The teacher approached us at the end of the course and encouraged us to sign up for the next level. "That dog has real potential."

I wish I could tell you that Shenzii is trained. I'd like to brag about how obedient and well-behaved she is. As long as she is in the back yard where I can get at her, Shenzii will do

> **SMARTEST AND DUMBEST DOGS**
>
> Most trainable breeds:
> Border collie, poodle, and German shepherd
>
> Least trainable breeds:
> Bulldog, Basenji, and Afghan hound
>
> —The Intelligence of Dogs

everything I tell her to do. "Sit," "Fetch," "Multiples of six."

But, occasionally, Shenzii escapes the back yard and runs amok in the neighborhood. She chases cats. She urinates in other people's yards. She pursues helpless automobiles down the middle of the road.

When she gets away, I can yell, "Sit," until I'm hoarse and she pays no attention. I shout, "Stay," "Come," "Heel"—all those commands she knows and obeys in the backyard—but I might as well be speaking Dalmatian. She acts as though she's stone deaf, and I'm reduced to chasing after her, breathing out murderous threats, and trying to keep my blood pressure under control.

At such times, it occurs to me that having a *mostly* obedient dog isn't much better than having a dog that doesn't obey at all. A half-trained dog just isn't worth much. If a dog won't submit to you when it

"Blessed are the meek, for they will inherit the earth."

matters, what good does it do if the dog submits perfectly all the rest of the time? Shenzii obeys me when it suits her. I don't think that's really obedience at all.

THE MISUNDERSTOOD MEEK
Christ offends us by calling on us to be meek.
—A. Herbert Gray

You have to be careful with words. They're living things. They grow and evolve and change. They mean one thing yesterday, another today, and still another tomorrow. You just can't put a word down and expect it to stay where you put it.

Where words really get us into trouble is when the same word comes to have multiple meanings. Take, for instance, the word "run." I can use that simple word to mean so many things, you won't have a clue what I'm talking about unless you pay close atten-

tion to the context. Am I referring to jogging, campaigning for public office, or an injury to your panty hose? Water can run. So can fish. There can be a run on certain items in the grocery store. I can use this word to describe how I feel (run down), or what I owe ("I've run up a bill"), or how things went at work ("I had a run-in with my boss"). I can run away even if I do so in a car rather than on my own two legs. I can run a shop or run guns or run around in circles while standing perfectly still. My nose can run. So can my mouth. Even Shenzii runs—but only when I yell, "Stay!"

Now if a word like run can be so mischievous, what do we do with a word like "meek"? It's not exactly a common word. We don't use it often in polite conversation. When Jesus says, "Blessed are the meek," we might tell ourselves we know exactly what he's talking about, but do we really? There's little context in the Beatitudes to help us discern what he intends by this word. And the word itself comes to us so tainted, so burdened with baggage, that we're almost guaranteed to misunderstand what Jesus is trying to tell us.

Once upon a time, the word meek (according to that revered, if stodgy, authority *The Oxford English Dictionary*) carried the sense of "gentle, courteous, kind. Free from haughtiness and self-will; piously humble and submissive; patient and unresentful under injury and reproach." (All that in such a short word!)

It's understandable, then, that the first translators of the Bible into English[1] would choose the word meek when translating Matthew 5:5.

At least, in their day, meek had a few virtuous overtones. But the fact that *modern* Bible translations (such as the *New International Version*) continue to choose this word is simple stubbornness. For meekness isn't what it used to be.

Swim back into the history of meek and you will discover that this word came to be used in an unfavorable sense (again, according to *Oxford*): "inclined to submit tamely to oppression or injury; easily put upon." Gradually, meek ceased to mean something virtuous to English speakers and, to the contrary, suggested something quite censurable.

Call someone meek today and they won't thank you. They may even feel insulted and attempt to hit you in the face! ("I'll show you how meek I am!")

Jesus blesses the meek. But we despise them. What's going on?

The word has changed meaning. What once denoted a lack of haughtiness has come to mean vacillating weakness. Ask most people today what this word means and they will tell you bluntly, "Meekness is a hat-in-hand, foot-shuffling, whatever-you-say demeanor that people with no confidence and

no self-respect adopt. Meekness is the 98-pound weakling who has no choice but to smile when someone kicks sand in his face. Meek people are mild, harmless, and ineffectual."

As Christians, we find ourselves on the horns of a dilemma with this word. On the one hand, we know what meekness means in the word-world in which we live. Frankly, we don't care for meekness any more than the next guy. But, on the other hand, we know Jesus pronounces a blessing on the meek. Matthew 5:5. There it is in black and white! Can't you read plain King James?

So how do we resolve the dilemma? We make a virtue out of the vice. We make "mild, harmless, and ineffectual" the Holy Trinity of Christian conduct. We elevate the role of the 98-pound weakling to saintly status. We paint Jesus with the

---

WEBSTER—SHMEBSTER

The Oxford English Dictionary (1933) is the authoritative and most complete reference work on the English language. It is thirteen volumes in length and contains more than 500,000 vocabulary entries.

THE SPINE OF A JELLYFISH

Actually, a jellyfish has no spine. They are classified as "invertebrates"—those land and sea creatures with no backbone. Worms and insects (and some politicians) fall into the same category.

— Microsoft Encarta

shoulders of a girl and the spine of a jellyfish. We renounce the forceful and eulogize the effeminate. We hold up as the epitome of discipleship the soft-spoken, timid, indecisive doormat the world despises—and, secretly, so do we.

And, having thus devalued this word, we evade the hard command that lies within it. Better to play the fop than to take seriously what Jesus means by meekness.

THE MEANING OF MEEK

The meek, the terrible meek, the fierce agonizing meek, are about to enter their inheritance.

—CHARLES RANN KENNEDY

The mistake Christians make with meekness is in failing to recognize one small change in the way the word came to be used. English speakers kept using meek to describe one person *in relation to another.* "She's too meek—people trample all over her." "What a meek man. He won't stand up to anybody." They (and eventually we) viewed meekness as a posture someone adopted when other people were present (subservient, one-down, docile). A person's "meekness quotient" was defined exclusively by how he or she behaved in the company of peers.

The secular world has the audacity to write God out of its language and exclude him from any definition of its words. But we shouldn't go to the Bible expecting such a thing to happen. Biblical concepts often require the presence of God to make sense—and to avoid being reduced to absurdities. So when you hear the word meek being used in Scripture, you should listen carefully to discern God in the word.

In the Bible, meekness has little to do with how we relate to others and much with how we relate to God. Certainly, there are times in Scripture when meekness describes a kind of behavior we show people around us. Paul commands us to deal with each other in "all lowliness and meekness."[2] But *interpersonal* behavior isn't the primary meaning for meekness—it's a by-product of true meekness.

Primarily, meekness is a posture we adopt in the presence of God. The humility and submissiveness implied by meekness is evidenced first and foremost in our demeanor before the Father. Meekness is surrender, abdication, and yielded obedience—but not the kind given by the weak to people who are stronger and more powerful. Meekness is bowing the knee to God. It's the surrender of self-will to God's will. It's the abdication of self-rule to God's rule. It's the commitment of spiritual pau-

GOD IN THE WORD?

It's easy to see how a word like "Goodbye" is based on "God." It is a contraction of "God be with you." But did you know that "God" is also the root of the word "gossip"? A "godsibb" was a person spiritually related to another, usually serving as a sponsor at baptism. [Today we would call such a person a godmother or godfather.] In time, however, a "gossip" came to mean a person with intimate knowledge of another and an eagerness to share that knowledge widely.

—**Webster's Word Histories**

pers and the brokenhearted to yield control to God.

So how do I know this is what Jesus means by meek in the third Beatitude? Because the Bible tells me so.

MEET TWO MEEK MEN

In every request, heart and soul and mind ought to supply the low accompaniment, "Thy will be done."

—GEORGE MACDONALD

Just as we met two characters in the New Testament who exemplified poverty, so too should we go to our Bibles to find examples of what God means by meek. There are just two people in the Bible who are specifically called meek. All of us are *encouraged* to be meek, but only two Bible characters (one in the Old Testament, one in the New) are singled out because they *epitomize* this trait. Perhaps we should look to their lives for help as we grapple with what meekness means.

I'm thinking about a man the Bible describes as "very meek, more than all men that were on the face of the earth"[3]—though you and I would not have called him a "meek man" had we met him. He was raised rich and powerful. He was accustomed to giving commands and having them instantly obeyed. He was prone to fits of anger. He once killed a man with his bare fists. He ordered hundreds of people put to death. He did not shrink from conflict or fear going toe-to-toe with people who didn't like him.

Moses was a merciful, meek man, and yet with what fury did he run through the camp, and cut the throats of three-and-thirty thousand of his dear Israelites that were fallen into idolatry.

—DANIEL DEFOE

This was no 98-pound weakling. This was no fearful, hand-wringing, indecisive doormat. This was no soft-spoken, diffident, timid soul who would never think of imposing or demanding or insisting. Moses was a powerful figure—strong-willed, bold, a leader. Yet God called him the meekest man on the face of the earth. Moses? Meek? Not if you go by our definition of meekness. But when you listen to how God defines meekness, it becomes clear why God saw this quality in Moses.

Though the meekness of Moses could be demonstrated by a number of incidents in his life, there was one defining moment that uniquely portrays what it means to be meek. It happened when Moses was eighty years old, and involved a burning bush, bare feet, and a disembodied voice. Remember? (Read Exodus 3–4 if you need to brush up on the story of Moses.) The interchange between God and Moses went something as follows (I paraphrase a bit):

God: Go. I am sending you to Pharaoh. Tell him, "Let my people go."

Moses: I don't want to go. He won't listen to me.

God: Go. Assemble the elders and tell them I sent you.

Moses: I don't want to go. They won't believe me.

God: Go. Command my people to come out of Egypt.

Moses: I don't want to go. I'm not a persuasive speaker.

God: Go. I will help you speak and teach you what to say.

Moses: I don't want to go. Please send someone else.

God: Go. Go anyway. Go because I told you to go. Go because I want you to go. Get up. Go now!

Moses: I don't want to go. But I will go because you command me. It's not what I want. But that's not really important. What you want is what matters most to me.

The way this little discussion concludes shows why God called Moses meek. It wasn't because he was particularly gentle with everyone around him or the kindest man alive. Certainly it wasn't because he was a wimp and let people walk all over him. Moses was meek because— knowing full well what he preferred, knowing what he would rather do, knowing his own desires and aspirations— he yielded to the will of God. When what he wanted and what God wanted went in different directions, Moses chose to walk God's way. He learned to say, "Not my will, but yours be done."

I'm thinking of another man the Bible calls meek. Actually, he was audacious enough to call himself meek.[4] We probably wouldn't have called him a meek man if we'd met him. He was forceful and opinionated. He demanded obedience of his followers. He railed against those who disagreed with him. He took on the religious and political powers of his day. He was so confrontive that, in the end, his enemies decided the only thing to do was get rid of him.

We cannot blink the fact that gentle Jesus meek and mild was so stiff in his opinions and so inflammatory in his language that he was thrown out of church, stoned, hunted from place to place, and finally gibbeted as a firebrand and a public danger.

—Dorothy Leigh Sayers

Once again, this was no 98-pound weakling. There was nothing indecisive or timid about the carpenter from Nazareth. Jesus was a powerful figure—bold and abrasive and supremely confident. Yet Jesus described himself as meek. Jesus? Meek? Not if you go by our definition of meekness. But when you listen to God's definition, it becomes clear why Jesus applies the term to himself.

Though the meekness of Jesus could be demonstrated by any number of incidents from his life, one defining moment portrays what true meekness is all about. It happened on the last night of his life, and involved some olive trees, three sleepy disciples, and an anguished prayer. Do you remember? (Read Matthew 26:36-46 if you need to brush up on Gethsemane.) The interchange between God and Jesus went something as follows (I paraphrase a bit):

God: Go. It's time for you to die.
Jesus: I don't want to go. There's so much more to do.
God: Go. It was for this reason I sent you.
Jesus: I don't want to go. There has to be another way.
God: Go. The soldiers are here.
Jesus: I don't want to go. We have swords. We can fight.
God: Go. Go anyway. Go because I told you to go. Go because I want you to go. Get up. Go now!
Jesus: I don't want to go. But I will because you command me. It's not what I want. But that's not really important. What you want is what matters most to me.

The way the prayer in Gethsemane concludes shows why Jesus could claim to be a meek man. It wasn't because he refrained from harsh words or refused to make hard judgments of the people around him. Certainly it wasn't because he rolled over every time someone differed with him. Jesus was meek because—knowing what he wanted, clear about what he preferred, aware of what he would like to do—he yielded to the will of God. When what he wanted and what God wanted went in different directions, Jesus took God's way. He, above all men, learned to say, "Not my will, but yours be done."

CLIMBING THE MOUNTAIN TO MEEKNESS

It is a very great thing to stand in obedience, to live under a superior, and not to be at our own disposal.
—THOMAS À KEMPIS

I know what Jesus means when he says, "Blessed are the meek," because I can look to Christ and Moses as examples of meekness. However, one clue in the Beatitudes themselves—a hint about the meaning of meekness—convinces me that meekness is about how we relate to God rather than how we interact with our friends and neighbors.

That hint is found in the way the Beatitudes are organized. We have already noted a *sequence* in these instructions—one leads to another, which leads to the next, and so on. But there is *structure* here as well—an organizing of the eight Beatitudes into two groups of four. If you look closely, you will see two distinct movements in these words: one leading us up to God, and one taking us back down to the real world.

THE SEVEN SUMMITS
The highest peaks on each of the seven continents are:
Everest (Asia)—29,028
Aconcagua (South America)—22,834
McKinley (North America)—20,320
Kilimanjaro (Africa)—19,340
Elbrus (Europe)—18,510
Vinson Massif (Antarctica)—16,067
Kosciusko (Australia)—7,316
—Into Thin Air

Through the remainder of this book, I make the assumption that the Beatitudes are built like a mountain.[5] The first four Beatitudes teach us how to behave toward God. The last four teach us how to act with each other. There is first an "ascent" into the presence of God and then a "descent" to the plane of daily life.

You can see this easily in the second group of Beatitudes. When Jesus blesses those who show mercy, make peace, and endure persecution, it's clear that he's talking about interpersonal skills—traits we use in relating to each other, not to God. God doesn't require our mercy; he makes peace with us (not vice versa); it's not God but people who persecute us. The second four Beatitudes, then, describe virtues disciples must develop as they deal with the people around them.

But the first four Beatitudes teach us the necessary skills to live in the presence of God. Poverty of spirit is what we experience when we see ourselves through God's eyes.

Mourning involves taking our sins as seriously as God does. Hungering for righteousness is developing an appetite for the things God loves. These first Beatitudes have to do with throne room behavior—how we interact with our King.

We'll play with this mountain metaphor throughout the book. And, at times, it will become an important tool for helping us interpret the meaning of a particular Beatitude. One of those times is now. What does Jesus mean by meekness here? Many writers want to define meekness interpersonally. They understand Jesus to say that disciples must be gentle and subservient as they deal with others.

I too believe disciples should be gentle and submissive, but that's not what I understand Jesus to be saying here with the third Beatitude. He's talking about a meekness that is God-directed, not people-directed. He is advocating a *vertical* virtue rather than a *horizontal* one.

These first four Beatitudes describe characteristics that are foundational for relating to God. A disciple must be humble (poor in spirit), broken (mourning), yielding (meek), and passionate for God (hungry). Beatitude meekness isn't about turning the other cheek or going the extra mile. It's about learning to say, "Not my will, but yours be done."

THE TAMING OF THE MEEK

All the natures of beastes and of byrdes and of serpentes and thynges of the see are meked and tamed of the nature of man.

—WILLIAM TYNDALE

The word translated meek was used by the Greeks to describe horses that were broken to the rein or haiter. There are few animals more proud, more powerful and fleet than horses. In their wild state, horses are beautiful and independent— but useless to humans. They can't be ridden. They won't haul a cart or pull a plow.

Oh, they have the strength. But they lack the *will*. Horses have an agenda of their own that doesn't include wearing a saddle or hauling a wagon. That's man-business. Horses would rather munch grass and roam free.

But take a horse and tame it, ride it until it submits, train it to the bridle and bit—and that horse becomes meek. It goes where you tell it to go. It does what you want it to do. Your agenda becomes its agenda. It lends its strength to helping you accomplish your work.

It's unfortunate that this process is called *breaking* a horse. Better to say the horse is tamed. The horse doesn't lose its strength by being domesticated. It doesn't suddenly become weak and timid and mild. A good horse has spirit even though it wears a saddle. All that has changed is that the horse and its strength is brought under control. It no longer demands to do what it wants.

The Greeks would say that such a horse is meek. The Christian might remark, "That

HORSEPOWER
James Watt (a Scottish inventor) studied the horse's ability to haul loads of coal. He determined that one horse could exert enough energy to lift 33,000 pounds by one foot in one minute. This became the standard measure of "horsepower."
— Microsoft Encarta

horse has learned to say, 'Not my will, but yours be done.'"

This is the picture that should come to mind when we think about meekness. Human beings—in our wild state—may be beautiful and powerful and proud. But we are useless to God. We won't be directed. We refuse to wear the bit. We do what we want to do when we want to do it.

Oh, we have the capacity to serve God. But we lack the *will*. There are things we prefer to do, which don't include listening to God and yielding to his desires. We know what we want. We pursue our own agendas.

But take those same humans and tame us—let God ride us until we submit, let him train us to godliness and the kingdom—and we too can become meek. We can learn to go where God tells us to go. We can do what God asks us to do. God's agenda becomes our agenda. We lend our strength to help-

ing God accomplish his work.

The world calls that kind of obedience being "broken, weak, spineless." No doubt they hope to ridicule Christians by debasing the word meek and then throwing it at us. But being tamed by God, yielding to his will, does not emasculate the Christian. We don't lose our strength and vigor and vitality. We don't suddenly become anemic and timid.

We simply become disciples. Our will is brought under his control. We are tamed to the purposes of God. We learn to say, "It's not what I want that is important. What you want is what matters most to me. Your will be done."

HALF-TAMED DISCIPLES

I spent much of the morning walking in the Park, and going to the Queene's chapell, where I staid and saw their masse, till a man came and bid me go out or kneel down: so I did go out.

—Samuel Pepys

We do struggle with meekness, don't we? It's hard to admit we are spiritual paupers. But if we live long enough, our failures will force that admission. It's difficult for us to mourn, though the consequences of sin eventually crash down upon us and compel regret.

But what makes us meek?

There are those who will admit themselves abominable wretches yet will never bend the knee to God. There are those who can weep an ocean of tears for their shame and folly and never yield to God's control. Many a Christian will start up the mountain toward God but will stumble at the very point where he or she is required to say, "What I want is not really important. What you want is what matters to me. Not my will, but yours be done."

Meekness takes more strength than many of us can muster.

Truth be told, the best of us are but half-meek. We're only partially broken, incompletely tamed to the purposes of God. Oh, we've been to obedience school. We've learned God's commands and can supply the required responses. So long as we're in the back yard, where God can get at us, we will follow Jesus anywhere.

But every so often, we slip our leashes and jump the fence. We escape to run amok for a while. We may not chase cats or urinate in other people's yards. But our behavior is just as uncontrollable and self-willed, as any dog on the lam from his master.

When those times occur, God can shout, "Sit," until he's hoarse. He can yell his commandments until he's blue in the face. But he might as well be speaking Hindu. We run wild and free—ignoring his demands and disobeying his will. And God runs after us pleading, "You're supposed to be my disciples. You've

promised to do my will. Why won't you obey?"

I wonder if God ever thinks that a *mostly* obedient disciple is not much better than someone who won't obey at all? Does it occur to him that half-tamed followers are more trouble than they're worth? Does he ever long to tell us that perfect submission *most* of the time isn't much good if a disciple won't submit when it matters?

Sometimes, as I'm chasing Shenzii, I grow ashamed. I think about how I obey God mostly when it suits me. Forgive me, Father. For that isn't really being obedient at all. And it certainly isn't being meek.

"I will be a saint" means I will despoil myself of all that is not God. . . . I will renounce my will, my inclinations, my whims and fancies, and make myself a willing slave to the will of God.

—Mother Teresa

TOP TEN . . .

TOP TEN LITTLE-KNOWN EXCUSES MOSES USED TO AVOID RETURNING TO EGYPT (AND, THUS, BEING MEEK)

10. My sheep dog is worthless away from the back yard.

9. Leaving Midian will void my Colonial Penn life insurance policy.

8. I'm eighty years old, for goodness sake! (What was your name again?)

7. I would go, Lord, but I've got a real phobia about bulrushes.

6. All that blowing sand keeps getting in my contact lenses.

5. It would take a burning bush to get me back to Egypt!

4. Pharaoh doesn't like me very much.

3. I'm scared of the aliens who built the pyramids.

2. I'll go, but only if Charlton Heston plays me in the movie version.

And the **#1** little-known excuse Moses used to avoid returning to Egypt:

This feeling keeps plaguing me that something bad will happen if I go back.

THE STORY OF . . .

Chuck Colson

BROKEN TO GOD

No one who knew Chuck Colson would have called him meek. Ambitious, driven, critical, ruthless—Colson was one of Richard Nixon's "hatchet men," the author of numerous dirty tricks during the Watergate era.

When the Watergate scandal brought down the Nixon administration, Colson was indicted, tried, and convicted of obstruction of justice. He served seven months in federal prison and was disbarred from the practice of law. For a man who had stood at the pinnacle of worldly power, a prison cell must have seemed a long fall from grace.

Yet, later Colson would say, "I really thank God for Watergate." For something else was happening to Colson during that difficult period—a very different kind of

conviction was taking place. Colson had been approached by a small circle of Christian men who befriended, prayed for, and taught the embattled public figure. For the first time, Colson was confronted by Christ and the Christian message. On the way home from a Bible study, Colson was overcome by his need and God's grace. Pulling to the curb while the tears flowed, this former "hatchet man" gave his life to Christ and was (in his words) "born again."

At his sentencing, Colson told the press, "I've committed my life to Jesus Christ," and humbly accepted the punishment meted out for his crimes. He served his prison time and then—slowly—began to put his life back together.

But it was a different kind of life. It focused not on the rich and powerful but on the outcasts of society. It centered on the Spirit rather than politics. And it was a life devoted to changing other

lives, rather than manipulating public policies and perceptions.

For the past twenty years, Colson has poured himself into Prison Fellowship—a ministry devoted to bringing the gospel to inmates and championing penal reforms. At present, this organization operates in hundreds of prisons across our nation and in more than fifty nations around the world.

Colson also ministers in other ways. He's an intense speaker who keeps a busy schedule of appearances with both Christian and civic groups. He records a popular radio program, "Break-Point." The ministry that has touched me personally has involved his writing. Author of a dozen books, including *The Body*, Colson has addressed contemporary issues regarding faith, ministry, and the community of Christ.

In a 1993 article on Colson in the *ABA Journal*,[6] one journalist remarked:

The interesting thing about Colson as a convert is that he hasn't changed that much. If you talk to him, you sense immediately that this is the kind of guy who indeed could have been and was one of the toughest and shrewdest political operatives in the United States. The only difference is his values . . . have been redeemed in an almost miraculous way.

Those who know him can verify this assessment of Colson. Even today, they would probably have difficulty calling him meek. He remains a driven, hard-hitting, intense individual. At an age when most men are thinking about retiring, Colson regularly wears out and replaces personal assistants in their twenties. He can still be impatient and demanding.

Yet, from the little I know of him, I would suggest that Colson is a good example of the Christian virtue of meekness. Notice the last sentence of the above quote: "The only difference is his values . . . have been redeemed in an almost miraculous way." I'd suggest that's a difference that makes all the difference. It's a difference demonstrating that Colson has learned to be meek.

Do you see the parallel to Moses' story? Powerful and positioned early in life. A rapid and scandalous fall. An exile to lonely places. A return to ministry among the misfits of society. Even a successful career as a writer! There's an intensity, a drive, an impatience in both these men that would disqualify each of them from being called meek—if we define that virtue as an interpersonal quality.

But, in Colson as in Moses, I see a man who exchanged selfish values for godly ones—someone seeking to say, "Not my will, but yours be done." People like Colson confront us with the idea that meekness is not the absence of ambition—but ambition for the kingdom rather than for self. Meekness is not a lack of drive—but an intensity placed at the service of the kingdom rather than self. Looking at Colson, it's possible to see that meekness is not weakness—it's strength put to use for God's purposes rather than our own.

Chuck Colson? Meek? Not if you go by the common definition of meekness. But when you listen to how *God* defines meekness—when you consider the meekness of Moses and even of Christ—then you begin to understand how the man once known as "the meanest man in Washington" might now be "the meekest man in Washington."

THINKING IT THROUGH

MONDAY

Our problem with "meekness" is that we have understood this word to describe how we relate to each other rather than to God. Meekness has become a horizontal quality rather than a vertical one. In contrast to that understanding, notice the following passages where the word "meekness" occurs (in the NIV).

- Read 1 Kings 21:20-29. Ahab "went around meekly" after hearing the prophet's judgment. Does this refer to the way he treated other people or to the fact that he "humbled himself before" God (verse 29)? What might this humbling involve?

- Read Psalm 37:1-11. Write out all the qualities that the psalmist uses to arrive at the phrase "the meek" (verse 11). Here, it's not *weakness* that's seen as the opposite of the meek, but what?

- Read 2 Corinthians 10:1-6. Notice how the "meekness of Christ" permits Paul to act with boldness, wage war, demolish strongholds, take captives, and punish. Does an understanding of meekness as *a consuming desire to do God's will* help you understand this passage better?

TUESDAY

Webster's Third New International Dictionary defines meek as

manifesting patience and long suffering; enduring injury without resentment; mild. Deficient in spirit and courage; submissive, tame. Not violent or strong; gentle, moderate, weak.

According to this understanding of meekness, Moses wouldn't have qualified. Look up the following passages and note how unlike the above definition Moses really was.

- Exodus 2:11-12,16-17; 11:4-8; 14:10-14; 32:15-20

- Numbers 11:10-15; 16:25-35

If, however, you define meekness as submission to God, it's evident why Moses should be called meek. How do the above passages demonstrate the meekness of Moses when meekness is understood as submission to God's will?

WEDNESDAY

In this chapter, we also looked at the life of Jesus for help in understanding what it means to be meek. In particular, we looked at the prayer in Gethsemane as an example of Jesus' submission to God's will. There are other examples too. Read the following passages and indicate how they demonstrate Christ's desire to be obedient to God.
Matthew 3:13-15; 26:50-54; John 4:34; 5:30; 6:38; 8:29; 12:27-28,49-50; 14:31; 19:28

THURSDAY

The notion that there's a structure to the Beatitudes that helps us interpret the parts by looking at the whole will become more important as we proceed, so spend a little time thinking about that structure. I proposed that the Beatitudes are built like a mountain: the first four describe "upward" qualities demonstrated to God, while the second four describe "downward," interpersonal qualities. With this in mind, think about the following questions:

- Do you have any doubt that the second half of the Beatitudes (especially "mercy," "peacemaking," and "persecution") describe interpersonal qualities? Do you see any way these Beatitudes might call us to be merciful to God, to make peace with God, to endure God's persecutions?
- In looking over the first four Beatitudes, does it seem likely to you that they describe characteristics we primarily demonstrate to God rather than our fellow human beings? If so, does the fact that "meekness" falls in the first half of the Beatitudes help you to see this as a vertical virtue rather than a horizontal one?

FRIDAY

Peter heard Jesus say, "Blessed are the meek." But, like us, Peter had a hard time submitting his will to the will of God. Read the following passages and comment on Peter's struggle to obey God rather than his own instincts or desires.

- Matthew 16:21-25; 26:31-35
- John 13:5-8; 18:10-11
- Acts 10:9-16
- Galatians 2:11-14

What was the most significant lesson you learned in your study this week?

TALKING IT OVER

TEXT: JONAH 1:1–3:5

WARM-UP:

Some things come easily to us. Others have to be learned. Name a talent or ability that comes naturally to you—something you were born with. Now tell the group about a skill you had to work at to develop.

Would you agree with the following statement? None of the Beatitudes comes naturally to us. Jesus is talking about *acquired* characteristics: they must be learned through painful struggle and over long periods of time.

Meekness is a word often used today to describe a certain personality type, a trait of weakness that comes naturally to certain people. In contrast, the Bible uses the word meek to speak of someone who is submitted to God, someone whose will has been yielded to God's. What do the examples of Moses and Jesus teach us about meekness?

Read Jonah 1:1–3:5, the famous story of Jonah, the "great fish," and the wicked city of Nineveh.

DISCUSSION:

Think about this story as the tale of a man who had to learn meekness.

1. What did God want Jonah to do? What did Jonah want to do? Whose will won out initially? At what point in this story does Jonah say, "Not your will, but *mine* be done?"

2. Notice the process God leads Jonah through as he teaches his prophet a bit of meekness. Do you see that God doesn't go straight to a lesson on submission and obedience? Jonah has a couple of other lessons to learn first. They sound surprisingly like the process Jesus describes in the Beatitudes.
   a. At what point in the story do you see Jonah learning to confess his poverty of spirit?
   b. Where in the story do you see Jonah learning to mourn and repent?

3. When is Jonah finally ready to demonstrate meekness?

4. Finally, Jonah is ready to do what God wants. What does Jonah do that clearly demonstrates he has learned to do God's will even when it conflicts with his own?

5. Why did God choose Jonah to begin with? Was there no one else in Israel who was more ready to obey his command? Or might it be that the sermon God was most interested in preserving through this book was not the one Jonah preached to Nineveh, but the one God preached to Jonah?

APPLICATION:

1. Tell the group about a time when you weren't very meek—a time when you told God, "Not your will, but mine be done."

2. Did God teach you anything about meekness in this incident? What "whale" did he send to swallow you? What finally brought you to the point where you could say, "Not my will, but yours be done?"

3. Is meekness a lesson we learn once, or does God keep

teaching us how to be meek? Just how many times do we have to be swallowed whole before we learn meekness for good?

4. Why do you think meekness comes so hard for us?
5. Do you think God ever longs to tell us that perfect submission *most* of the time isn't much good if a disciple won't submit when it matters?

COOL DOWN:

It's easy to obey God when we agree with him. What's hard is obeying him when we don't want to. It doesn't take much of a commitment to follow Jesus everywhere *we* want to go. Real commitment (and real meekness) is a matter of saying "yes" when you would rather say "no."

If you had one piece of advice to give the group on "how to obey God when it hurts," what would it be?

Take Jonah's prayer (Jonah 2:2-9) and pray it together as a group as you bring your time to a close.

LIVING IT OUT

The chapter "The Discipline of Submission" in Richard Foster's wonderful book *Celebration of Discipline* provides a helpful structure for applying meekness in our lives. Listen to Foster's recommendation:

At the beginning of the day we wait before Father, Son and Holy Spirit, in the words of the hymn writer, "yielded and still." The first words of our day form the prayer of Thomas à Kempis, "As thou wilt; what thou wilt; when thou wilt." We yield our body, mind and spirit for his purposes. Likewise the day is lived in deeds of submission interspersed with constant ejaculations of inward surrender. As the first words of the morning are of submission so are the last words of the night. We surrender our body, mind and spirit into the hands of God to do with us as he pleases through the long darkness.[7]

In Foster's view, submission to the will of God runs so counter to our natural inclinations that only a day bathed in prayer and constant promises of obedience can create an obedient mindset. He recommends prayer to begin, carry us through, and end our day.

I like that notion. For one week (or two or twenty!), why not begin every day with the following regimen? The first step involves a little prayer and study before jumping into your hectic routine.

Father,
I confess that I am only half-tamed to your will. How grateful I am for those parts of my life that you have brought under your control. How sorry I am for pieces of myself I have not yielded to you.

Lord, today I will be tempted to slip your leash and live as I please. Grant me the strength to resist that temptation. Help me to live this day in obedience. Show me how you want me to think and feel and behave as I go through my day. Let me live free of myself and in submission to you.

"As thou wilt; what thou wilt; when thou wilt. Amen."

Follow this prayer with a few minutes' reading and memorizing God's Word. It does little good to pray for obedience if you don't know what God's will is for your life! Spend some time each day educating yourself in the ways of God. The following passages might be particularly useful for keeping your life centered on God's will: Matthew 5:3-16; John 14:15-21; Romans 6:1-4,11-14; 8:5-14; 1 Corinthians 13:4-8; Galatians 5:16-25; Ephesians 4:17–5:2; 6:13-18; Philippians 2:1-11; 4:4-9; Colossians 3:1-17; 1 Peter 1:13-19; 4:7-11; 2 Peter 1:5-11; 1 John 5:1-4.

The second step involves reminding yourself of this commitment to obedience throughout the day. I suggest you adapt the prayer of Thomas à Kempis, repeating frequently and with feeling: As you will, what you will, when you will. I have a colored dot on my watch that reminds me of my commitment to obedience and prompts me to pray this prayer. You might want to tape this prayer to the bathroom mirror and to the dashboard of your car and to your desk at work. Put the prayer in places where you're tempted to "run amok" — on the television or computer screen, the refrigerator door, the telephone. Keeping in mind that we are disciples *all the time* is half the battle with obedience.

Finally, end your day with prayer. Kneeling at the side of the bed before sleep might not be your habit, but it's not a bad habit to develop. Try kneeling and saying a prayer like this:

Father,
I felt your power today. I found in you the strength to say "no" and to resist temptation. I felt you prompting me to say and do godly things. [You might want to name a specific example here.] I'm so grateful for your constant presence in my life. Thank you for training me to be meek.

But, Father, I also felt the power of my own will. There were times today when my stubbornness and pride welled up and persuaded me to go my own way. [You might want to name a specific example here.] Forgive me for wanting my will more than yours.

Tomorrow is a fresh day. I lie down with gratitude for your presence with me today. I joyfully anticipate your presence with me tomorrow. Make me meek, O Lord, more and more yielded to your perfect will. Amen.

IN A WORD

Meekness is the willingness to say, **"I will submit to God."** It's a commitment to obedience that's tested most when what we want diverges from God's desires for us. Submitting when it counts is the litmus test of discipleship.

Hungering FOR GOD

Lord thy most pointed pleasure take and stab my spirit broad awake;
Or Lord if too obdurate I Choose thou before that spirit die
a piercing pain a killing sin And to my dead heart run them in.

—ROBERT LOUIS STEVENSON

t's perhaps the saddest story in Scripture. There are two sisters in the tale—one "lovely in form, and beautiful,"[1] the other, not. The older sister had "weak [perhaps crossed?] eyes"; she was well on her way to becoming an old maid when first we meet her. But the younger sister was striking enough to make a grown man cry.[2] (If you haven't read about Leah and Rachel lately, you might want to scan Genesis 29.)

As fate would have it, both were destined to marry the same husband, but for very different reasons. Jacob was mad about Rachel from the moment he set eyes on her. He yearned for her. He was in love with her[3] and gave seven years of his life to make her his wife. But "they seemed like only a few days to him because of his love for her."[4]

Before Jacob could marry Rachel, he was tricked into marrying Leah—whom he didn't want. He hadn't given the best years of his life for the privilege of her company. Jacob was incensed that her father had taken advantage of dark and drink to slip this ugly duckling into Jacob's bed. "What is this you have done to me? . . . Why have you deceived me?"[5]

Do you remember how the story ends? Jacob marries Rachel too. Both sisters live out their days in Jacob's tents.

THE NUMBERS ON MARRIAGE

Believe it or not, 93 percent of Americans will marry at some point in their lives. Yet there's one divorce every twenty-six seconds. Three-fourths of adults under thirty believe it's either hard or impossible to have a good marriage these days.

— www.smartmarriage.com

Jacob does his husbandly duty toward each of them, providing them with shelter and clothing. He doesn't deny either of them their conjugal rights. Their children are cared for and blessed. There's no indication that Jacob abused or mistreated Leah.

But Jacob never loved Leah. He met his responsibilities to her and honored the commitment forced upon him. But there was no enthusiasm, no passion, no hunger to their relationship. It was marriage by the numbers as far as Jacob and Leah were concerned.

PANTING FOR GOD?

The true measure of loving God is to love him without measure.

—ST. BERNARD OF CLAIRVAUX

The way things stand between this husband and wife reminds me of the kind of relationship many of us have with faith. The relationship is polite and proper and pragmatic. We do our duty and honor our com-

mitments. But there's little in the way of passion in our religious experience. Faith is our Leah.

We wake up one day to realize the religion we married was not what we thought it was. Lying there beside us is a set of propositional truths we pledged allegiance to. We've been coupled to a list of facts and accurate answers to theological questions. But, with the coming of morning, it dawns on us that correct beliefs don't necessarily result in passionate believing. It's one thing to profess faith, another thing to care deeply about what you profess. It's possible to marry faith, but still not love her.

Often, what drives this point home is running into someone whose faith is a Rachel. Once in a while, we come across people who are genuinely "mad" about their walk with God. They yearn for his presence. They are deeply, obviously "in love" with him. They reserve the best of themselves for their relationship with their Lord.

Such meetings are always disorienting for us. We stumble across a believer who has a fire in the belly, and it makes us nervous. We bump into a Christian who has a constant sense of suppressed zeal—a fervor that spills out in worship or witness or some extravagant deed—and we feel oddly threatened. We find this person's ardor attractive, yet suspicious. We want to ask, "Why are you so passionate for God?" But we're afraid that—in asking the question—we may be telling more about ourselves than we care to reveal.

*As the deer pants for
    streams of water, so my soul
    pants for you,
O God. My soul thirsts for God,
    for the living God.*[6]

We meet this kind of person, with this kind of faith, in the pages of the Bible. God's sacred story is peopled with characters who possessed this sort of religious fervor, this hunger for God. Have you ever read through the Psalms

"Blessed are those who hunger and thirst for righteousness, for they will be filled."

and come upon David's longing-filled poem?

Panting? Thirsting? What is David talking about here? I'm knowledgeable about God. I even try to be obedient to God. But rarely do I breathe heavily in anticipation of meeting with him. Seldom do I feel parched for his presence. David, what do you have that I lack?

Have you read Philippians and stubbed your toe on Paul's intemperate, fervent proclamation?

But whatever was to my profit I now consider loss for the sake of Christ. What is more, I consider everything a loss compared to the surpassing greatness of knowing Christ Jesus my Lord, for whose sake I have lost all things. I consider them rubbish, that I may gain Christ. . . .[7]

Rubbish? Surpassing greatness? What is Paul talking about? I've said "no" to a few things as I try to follow the

Lord. I appreciate Jesus as much as the next guy. But I find it difficult to get so excited about him that I let go of everything else in my life, considering it rubbish in comparison. Paul, what do you experience in your relationship with God that I don't?

Or have you ever happened across Jeremiah's reluctant passion?

[If I say to myself] "I will not mention him or speak any more in his name," his word is in my heart like a fire, a fire shut up in my bones. I am weary of holding it in; indeed, I cannot.[8]

His word is like a fire? I can't hold it in? What is Jeremiah talking about? I find it all too easy *not* to mention God or speak in his name. There's no compelling urge, no fire in my bones, to break out in witness.

What was it in Jeremiah

that motivated such a burning, consuming desire for God?

We look at these people and find their yearning, their longing for God, bewildering—and profoundly convicting. Confronted with such passion, faced with an experience of God that goes deeper and touches something more powerful than memorized creeds and vague theological dogmas, our own spiritual walk seems cold and by-the-numbers in comparison. As we consider that kind of passionate faith, we're not content to say, "I don't get it." We want to push through our religious reserve to experience the same kind of fervor they felt. We want a little fire ourselves. You and I could use a healthy dose of passion for the things of God.

Welcome to the fourth Beatitude.

FROM THE PITS TO THE PEAK

In the last chapter, we discovered that the Beatitudes are structured like a mountain. The first half of discipleship involves an ascent—turning our backs on the pit of self and making the long, hard climb up the mountain to the pinnacle of God. Let's review what we've seen in the Beatitudes so far.

We began this journey as self-involved, self-centered sinners. Like eternal two-year-olds, our world revolved around the sun of self—our wants, our needs, our way. We were proud, defiant, self-willed, and passionate about nothing so much as "me."

Then came the initial, faltering steps of discipleship. Seeing ourselves for the first time—not as others see us and certainly not as we want to see ourselves, but as God sees us—we faced ourselves squarely and without excuse. Our "searching moral inventory" left us battered and deeply wounded. We confessed ourselves as sinners and admitted that we were beggars from a God's-eye perspective.

As confession led to mourning, we began the painful process of turning away from self and toward God. In grief and shame, so sickened by self that we could no longer bear it, we wept for our poverty and renounced the self-willed, self-directed, self-sufficient life. We repented of our sins, owning them fully and grieving them deeply.

Only then were we ready for the climb to meekness, orienting ourselves toward the one who alone can teach us, train us, and break us to a will other than our own. In submission, we learned to say, "Not my will, but yours be done."

Now, at last, we arrive at the pinnacle of the Beatitudes.

Blessed are the people who yearn for the things of God. Happy are those whose appetites, obsessions, and fondest desires are fixed on the King and his kingdom. How wonderful it is to desire righteousness like the starving hunger for food and the parched thirst for water.

Martin Luther, in his commentary on the Sermon on the Mount, defined this appetite for the holy as

. . . a hunger and thirst for righteousness that can never be curbed or stopped or sated, one that looks for nothing and cares for nothing except the accomplishment and maintenance of the right, despising everything that hinders this end.[9]

Martyn Lloyd-Jones summed up the fourth Beatitude in this manner:

To hunger and thirst after righteousness is to desire to be free from self in all its horrible manifestations, in all its forms. . . . [It is] the longing to be positively holy.[10]

In short, what Jesus blesses here are those who have learned to be passionate about holy things. He describes a relationship between disciples and the ways of God in which words like panting, longing,

HUNGER

Worldwide, 841 million people are chronically undernourished. In developing countries, 34 percent of children under the age of five are undernourished. In the United States, 11 million people are estimated to go hungry each year.

—www.bread.org

desire, and zeal can be used meaningfully. He speaks to the possibility that faith can be our Rachel.

THE PROBLEM WITH PASSION

The knowledge of God is very far from the love of him.
—BLAISE PASCAL

If you're like me, you find yourself caught with this Beatitude. On one hand, Jesus blesses those who hunger for God. On the other, my appetite for God isn't as keen as it needs to be. How can we develop a raging thirst and a passionate hunger for righteousness?

We're tempted to think that our problem with this Beatitude is a problem of the *head*—if only we better understood what Jesus was saying, we might feel what Jesus is blessing. So we pull out our dictionaries and commentaries and concordances—and do to this Beatitude the one thing that kills it. We take a statement meant to transform us and turn it into another of those nice sayings by that nice man Jesus.

Put that dictionary down! We already know what Jesus means when he talks about righteousness. Oh, we may not be able to toss off a definition that would make Webster smile, but we understand enough about righteousness to know that our greatest need is not for more precise definitions. Whatever the details might be, Jesus is talking here about living in a way that pleases our heavenly Father.

Forget the commentaries! We already know more than we care to admit about hunger and thirst. We're all too familiar with obsessions, cravings, appetites, and yearnings that gnaw us to distraction. Every one of us has wanted something so badly we could taste it.

Our problem with this Beatitude is not a failure to understand the words themselves. Our problem is that we so rarely use these words *together* in the same sentence.

Righteousness is one thing. Passion is another. But being passionate about righteousness? Panting for God? You might as well talk about love and Leah.

"Blessed are those who hunger and thirst for righteousness" is a Beatitude directed at our hearts. It asks not what we know, but what we feel. Jesus doesn't inquire if we can *define* righteousness but whether we *desire* it. He already knows we have passions; what he wants to know is whether we have any passion for *the things of God*.

And that is a confrontational question! It strikes at the heart of the tepid Christianity too many of us practice. There's a brand of faith that makes us subject to the commands of God, but permits little joy and zeal and fervor in obeying them. There's a kind of discipleship that breeds enough commitment to get us to church on Sunday, but fails to light a consuming fire within us through the

OTHER OXYMORONS
bittersweet
jumbo shrimp
old news
same difference
working vacation

week. There's a form of religion that sparks in us a semblance of holiness—but, too often, it's a semblance devoid of life-changing power. It's faith by the numbers, discipleship by the book, religion as Leah.

That kind of faith will generate only enough heat to make us do our duty. We'll provide for it, take care of it, even defend it. But we don't love it. It's not the passion of our lives.

TWO HAZARDS ON THE WAY TO THE TOP

The way to avoid evil is not by bemoaning our passions, but by compelling them to yield their vigour to our moral nature.

—HENRY WARD BEECHER

Christians I know tend to do one of two things with this Beatitude—both of them dangerous. Either they try to begin discipleship with the hunger for righteousness or they settle for a discipleship that stops just short of passion.

Some Christians (who can't really identify with a lack of passion for God, who already feel what they claim to be a great yearning for holy things) are tempted to *start* discipleship at the fourth Beatitude. They loudly proclaim their love for righteousness. But they don't care for poverty, they don't like tears, and they aren't enamored with meekness. "Can't we just skip the first three Beatitudes and go right to the summit of it all?"

These Christians seem to be looking for a short-cut up the mountain of discipleship. They want a holy helicopter to transport them past all the messy stuff and drop them off where the fourth Beatitude takes up. "I love righteousness! No one is more passionate about being right than I am. Take me straight to the presence of God!"

Now, it's true that you can hunger for *self*-righteousness without climbing through the first three Beatitudes. (The Pharisees are

proof of that. They were hungry for a holiness of sorts.) But the hunger Jesus recommends is an acquired taste. A craving for *God's* righteousness requires that you first face your own emptiness. An appetite for the holy is only possible when you cleanse the palate of self. Discipleship must begin with poverty and tears if it's ever to reach genuine hunger for God.

But it is the second danger most of us should be concerned about—the overwhelming temptation to settle for a discipleship that never quite makes it to hunger. Having scaled as high as meekness, many of us decide to set up camp and consider our climb complete. Submission is as far as we go. Faith is forever Leah.

Oh, we'll give faith her due. We resign ourselves to obedience. We grit our teeth and yield to God's commands. We reach deep inside and muster enough

APPETITE CAN KILL
Some 7,000 people die from food poisoning in the United States every year, and another 7 million get ill from eating contaminated food.
—USDA

self-discipline and sheer determination to stay on the straight and narrow. We'll do what's *required* of a disciple. But there's not much eagerness, not a great deal of joy, not a whole lot of passion about it.

We get stuck at meekness and imagine that we've arrived. We plant our flag on the false summit of submission, unaware that there's one more step leading beyond duty to passion.

Meekness is a wonderful thing—it teaches us to submit to God. But it was never meant to be the final word on discipleship. Meekness is needed to lead us to say, "Your will—not mine—be done." But God never intended our will and his to be forever in conflict. Meekness is necessary; it breaks us so we do what we *ought to*. But it takes more than meekness—it takes hunger—to transform *ought to* into *want to*.

Unrelieved by a passion for godliness, meekness makes obedience a chore. We take our minimum daily dosage of righteousness, but the minimum is about all the righteousness we can stand. Morality becomes medicinal. Holiness becomes duty. Christianity becomes a marathon of obligation instead of the joyous, transformative, empowering faith God intended.

Is that all there is to discipleship? No! When Jesus blesses hungering and thirsting for righteousness, he speaks of a level of Christian living where gritting is transformed into panting, where the pain in the neck becomes a fire in the belly, where a hunger for the things of God grows so compelling we can say with the prophet of old:

When your words came,
  I ate them;
they were my joy and my heart's
  delight. . . .[11]

> ## BORING!
> Since 1984, Alan Caruba has polled people across the country to learn what they find monotonous.
> ### THE TOP TEN:
> Standing in line, laundry, commuting, meetings, diets, exercise, yardwork, housework, political debates, and junk mail.
> —The Boring Institute

A RULING PASSION

And hence one master-passion
  in the breast,
Like Aaron's serpent, swallows
  up the rest.

—ALEXANDER POPE

I'm asking you to get off your meekness, brush away your fatigue, and climb that last stretch with me to spiritual passion. To do that, you need to know one more thing about the route ahead. When Jesus speaks of a "hunger for righteousness," he's not talking about one hunger among many. He's talking about a *ruling* hunger, a "master-passion" that swallows up all the rest.

You hear it clearly in his statements about righteousness through the remainder of the Sermon on the Mount. This hunger for righteousness is so profound, it can't be beaten out of disciples—they will suffer persecution rather than give it up.[12] It's a hunger that goes beyond anything the meticulous Pharisees ever experienced.[13] It's a hunger that doesn't depend on an audience—disciples are ravenous for God even in their closet and in their secret deeds.[14]

It's a hunger that causes us to seek first the kingdom of God, trusting that all other hungers will be taken care of when we do.[15]

Jacob had such a hunger. It was Rachel. For the sake of his passion for her, he gave up years of his life, worked his fingers to the bone, suffered physically and financially, and sublimated every other desire to the goal of making her his wife. Jacob would sacrifice anything on the altar of Rachel.

Jesus says it's possible to promote righteousness to a master passion, a ruling hunger. He suggests that disciples can be so consumed with a love for God and the things of God that all else is sacrificed to the pursuit of that one holy hunger. Self, sin, power, fame, money— it's possible to come to a point where nothing can compete with the single-minded pursuit of the King and his kingdom.

Jesus paints a picture of discipleship that many of us want, but few of us experience. Think about a motivation for righteousness stemming from appetite rather than obligation. Think of a kind of discipleship in which holy living is no longer a chore that runs counter to your real desires, but a ruling passion that overwhelms all other desires. Imagine developing such a taste for the things of God that you can't get enough, can't do enough, can't gorge on God enough to satisfy your longing. Imagine waking up every morning to Rachel.

In a religious milieu where so many have apparently lost their taste for righteousness, the notion of hungering again for the holy is striking. In the midst of people who seem to have as much righteousness as they can stand, the idea of thirsting for more is remarkable. I'm weary of Christianity devoid of appetite. I'm tired of discipleship that talks much of self-control but very little of the uncontrollable craving to do right. I'm exhausted by faith that addresses the head but neglects the heart. I want a Rachel kind of faith.

HUNGERING FOR HUNGER

Only great passions can elevate the soul to great things.
—Denis Diderot

I'm overwhelmed by a great sadness for Leah. I can close my eyes and imagine the first look this bride received from her husband the morning after their marriage was consummated—stunned shock dissolving into deep disappointment. I think about how wounded she must have been, and how she continued to hurt through the years, resigned to the fact that the only husband she would ever have didn't truly love her.

I wonder if God ever feels that from me. Does he know that he often takes a back seat to other interests? Does he sense that I have other passions that compete with my love for him? I'm afraid that I give God plenty of cause to feel like Leah. I don't hunger for him as he wants me to. I'm not as passionate about him as I should be. I know I'm supposed to be zealous and enthusiastic and eager, but I seem to yawn a whole lot more than I pant. Righteousness is not the ruling passion of my life.

And God knows it. He sees it in my eyes every morning and in my deeds every day.

We think this Beatitude is telling us that, once we develop an appetite for righteousness, God will "fill" us with the righteousness we desire. If we provide the passion, God will provide the piety.

But that's precisely the problem. How can Jesus demand passion? How can he require desire? You can't order someone to love chocolate ice cream, much less righteousness. If you don't have a hunger

for God, how do you get it? If God is your Leah, how can he become your Rachel?

The great irony, of course, is that God is *not* Leah. He is neither ugly nor undesirable. He is not the one with "weak eyes." We are. Our God is beautiful beyond imagining. Those who have seen him have been struck dumb (some have even been struck *dead*) by his beauty. Our lack of passion for God indicates nothing about discerning tastes and everything about spiritual blindness.

And, of course, the things we feel such passion for (our vices, our treasures, our selves) are no Rachel. We're spending our lives in love with warted hags. We embrace repulsive crones, too blind to see what we're holding . . . and what is holding us.

What are such hopelessly confused people to do?

Try asking God to do something to us.

Like the fellow who told Jesus, "I

do believe; help me overcome my unbelief,"[16] there are times when all we can do is tell God, "I do love you; help me love you better!" We can hunger to be hungry. We can want to want him. But left to ourselves, a passion for God is always just out of reach.

We already know that God alone can make us righteous. What we really need is for God to also make us hungry. It's going to take divine intervention to spark in us a passion for godly things. The God who raises us from the dead will need to fill our dead hearts with zeal for him. When God promises in this Beatitude to "fill" us, he intends to start first with appetite before he works on righteousness.

When I think of it that way, I'm encouraged. When I consider that God is as eager for me to love him as I am, I find hope. I'm not climbing this mountain alone. God is not only my goal—he's my companion on the journey. What I lack, God will provide. He'll fill me with hunger so that he

TOP FIVE ICE CREAM FLAVORS

Nearly 30 percent of the ice cream eating public prefer vanilla, compared to 9 percent who favor chocolate, 5 percent who choose butter pecan or strawberry, and 4 percent for neopolitan. My favorite, mint chocolate chip, garnered less than 1 percent of the vote.

—International Ice Cream Association

can fill me with righteousness.

So how do I become God's partner in that process?

Consider Jacob and Leah once more. What if Jacob had approached Leah one day and confessed, "Leah, I don't love you as I should"? What if he'd told her he wanted to love her better? What if he'd admitted that the problem was him, not her? What if he'd begged for her forgiveness and asked for her help? What if he'd determined that nothing, not even Rachel, was going to keep him from falling head over heels for Leah?

I don't think Leah would have scorned such an approach. In fact, she probably would have responded with real excitement and tangible assistance. She would have done all in her power to grow a love for herself in her husband.

Will God do less if we approach him in a similar way? We may not hunger for God as we should, but we can confess that to him. We can tell him we long to love him better. We can admit that the problem is in ourselves—in our skewed values, in our fallen viewpoints—rather than in him. We can beg his forgiveness and ask for his help.

We can determine that nothing—neither sin nor self nor Satan himself—will keep us from panting for God.

I know how God will respond to that. He won't scorn or refuse us. He'll run to meet us and throw his arms around us and kiss us passionately. He'll shower us with his affection. He will pour out his blessings on us. God will do all in his power to grow a love for himself in his disciples.

God doesn't need to see a raging passion within us to fill us with every good thing. All he needs is a willing flicker he can fan into a flame.

TOP TEN . . .

TOP TEN UNEXPECTED RESULTS OF HUNGERING FOR RIGHTEOUSNESS

10. You find you can go back for seconds without a twinge of guilt.

9. Unleavened bread and grape juice replace dairy products as your favorite food group.

8. You discover that the fruit of the Spirit is more satisfying than chips and salsa.

7. You have to let out several more notches in your Belt of Truth.

6. People notice that you seem full of something other than yourself.

5. For the first time in your life, you secretly long for people to call you "Fatty."

4. The last time you went to Kentucky Fried Chicken, you tried to order the "Breastplate of Righteousness."

3. Stuffing yourself results in a different kind of heartburn.

2. You look forward to the day when you have to shop in the Big and Tall section of your local Christian bookstore.

And the **#1** unexpected result of hungering for righteousness:

You develop a strange craving for locusts and wild honey.

THE STORY OF...

A PASSION FOR GOD

I wanted this section of each chapter to portray a real person who exemplified the Beatitude under consideration. And I did think of a few people to profile as examples of hungering for righteousness—Augustine, St. Francis of Assisi, or Billy Graham, for example. But perhaps this is one Beatitude best served by contrast rather than by illustration.

We live in a culture that feels great passion about tiny things. Our appetites have grown debased. Our tastes are common and vulgar. We hunger for junk food of the body, mind, and soul.

Americans understand how to be passionate about sports. Athletes will give up years of their lives, subsist at poverty level, rise early to train in rain or snow, restrict their diets, push their bodies to painful limits, consult sports psychologists, endure injuries and fatigue, and sacrifice relationships, careers, and any other vestige of a normal life—all to satisfy their craving for Olympic gold or world records. The rest of us will run cable to our homes, buy a big-screen TV, install surround-sound, sign up for pay-per-view, and spend countless hours in front of the tube—so great is our appetite to watch those athletes perform. We'll drive for many miles to a multi-million-dollar stadium, pay exorbitant parking and ticket prices, and (to add insult to injury) pay five dollars for a hot dog that should cost fifty cents—just for the pleasure of seeing some overdeveloped millionaire hit a ball or make a tackle. Such a vast appetite for such a trivial thing.

And we understand what it means to be hungry for sex. We spend billions of dollars annually on creams, ointments, perfumes, make-up, and lotions to make ourselves more attractive and alluring. We diet and exercise and endure plastic surgery to keep our bodies trim and sexy. A starlet—whose sole asset involves a set of genes resulting in pleasing arrangements of features and body parts—will be paid millions of dollars to undress before the greedy camera because Hollywood knows we'll pay even more millions for the privilege of watching her do so. Men will give up wives, children, savings, reputation, career, and self-respect to quench their thirst for another woman. Women will destroy their families and futures to feed their craving to be desired. We're obsessed with skin and careless about character.

We're even passionate about hobbies. Fishing, model airplane building, painting, woodworking, golfing, collecting—the list could go on for pages. Americans are a people desperate to fill up their spare time with mindless and expensive diversions. We squander vast quantities of time, money, and attention on the most trivial of pursuits. The average American male gives more time and attention to the hobby of his choice than to his children.

Yes, we know what it means to be passionate. It's just that our passions revolve around tiny and unworthy things. We give the best of ourselves to matters that, ultimately, don't matter. Our hungers degrade rather than elevate us.

Where are the people among us who hunger to this degree for righteousness? Where are the contemporary saints who go to the same lengths for holy things that so many others go to for sports? Why can we name so many who are passionate for baseball or physical beauty or fly

fishing, but so few who are starving for God?

In fact, I believe there are hundreds (thousands!) of people in our land who are hungry for righteousness. We just don't know about them. Our culture doesn't hold such people in high regard. They don't make heroes out of men and women who are passionate about doing right and becoming godly people. You won't see them interviewed on "20/20." They won't be invited to the White House.

Yet they are among us. Some of them are single parents raising their children in the "paths they should go"—even though they must fight against overwhelming odds to do so. Some are business people who have come to view their businesses and profits as opportunities for ministry rather than vehicles for personal enrichment. Some are husbands and wives, whose commitments

to each other and to God transcend whatever struggles or temptations they may face. Some are teens who are trying to submit themselves to parents who don't know Jesus and don't love spiritual things. And more than a few of them are pastors who are giving their lives to pursuing God and serving his people.

So instead of naming one individual who personifies a hunger for righteousness, I thought I might ask you to fill in the blank. Do you know someone who is passionate for holiness, who craves to live like Jesus, who hungers for the right? Is there someone you could name whose most burning appetite seems to be for God and his ways? If so, put his or her name in the space at the right, tear out these pages, and give them to that person with your thanks.

And one more thing. Hug that person for me.

Someone I know who is passionate for righteousness.

THINKING IT THROUGH

MONDAY

In this chapter, we noted some examples of people who had a consuming passion for the things of God—David, Paul, Jeremiah. There were other examples we could have observed. Read the following passages and write down: (1) how each person demonstrated a passion for God, and (2) what you learn about your own walk with God from their zeal.

- Numbers 25:1-13—The story of Phinehas
- Job 1:1–2:12—The story of Job
- 2 Kings 23:1-25 (especially verse 25)—The story of Josiah
- Daniel 6:1-16—The story of Daniel
- John 2:12-17—The story of Jesus in the temple

TUESDAY

Unfortunately, for every example of someone who hungered for God, there are probably ten examples of people who hungered for other things. Again, read the following passages, note the "ruling passion" of the person mentioned, and reflect on the ways other hungers compete with a passion for God.

- Joshua 6:17-19; 7:1-26 (especially verse 21)—The story of Achan
- 1 Kings 11:1-6 (especially verse 2)—The story of Solomon
- Matthew 6:1-6,16-18; 23:1-6—The story of the Pharisees
- Mark 10:17-22—The story of the rich young man
- Acts 8:9-25—The story of Simon the Sorcerer

WEDNESDAY

We looked at two hazards that confront us as we approach this Beatitude. The first of these is the desire to start discipleship at the fourth Beatitude—avoiding the bother and the messiness of the first three. No one was more intent on being righteous than the Pharisees. But the Pharisees we meet in the Gospels have little interest in confessing sin or submitting their hearts to God. The following passages indicate some of Jesus' problems with the Pharisees. Read them carefully and indicate which of the first three Beatitudes Jesus accuses the Pharisees of skipping.

- Matthew 6:5-6
- Matthew 13:38-41
- Matthew 15:1-9
- Matthew 23:23-28
- Luke 16:13-15
- Luke 18:9-14

THURSDAY

The second hazard we're likely to encounter at this point in the Beatitudes is the temptation to settle for a discipleship that never quite makes it to hunger. Below are some passages that focus on people (or groups) who seem to fall into this category. Read the passages, indicating who is being talked about and how their lack of passion for God is evidenced.

- Jeremiah 7:1-11
- Amos 5:21-24
- Luke 7:36-50
- John 6:24-27,35-36
- 2 Timothy 3:1-6
- Revelation 3:14-16

FRIDAY

Throughout this chapter, we've been talking about passion. But not raw passion. Fervor must always be informed by principle, the heart controlled by the mind. Notice how God (through the following passages) warns us about unbridled passion or, as Paul terms it, zeal "not based on knowledge." Write down who is being talked about as "zealous," what danger their zeal posed, and the advice given in contrast.

- Proverbs 19:2
- Romans 10:1-3
- Galatians 1:13-14; Philippians 3:6
- Galatians 4:17-18

TALKING IT OVER

TEXT: LUKE 7:36-50

WARM-UP:

Passion will lead you to do extravagant, foolish, even dangerous things. Share with the group something you've done "for love" that now seems overboard or rash. What is it about passion that makes all of us a bit extreme?

Do you have a similar story to tell about doing something extravagant, foolish, or dangerous because of a passion for God? Has your love for God ever made you a bit extreme? If so, share that with the group too.

In Luke's gospel, we're introduced to a woman who behaved extravagantly because she loved Jesus with all her heart. Read Luke 7:36-50.

DISCUSSION:

1. Doesn't it seem likely that the woman had met Jesus before? What if she were the woman caught in adultery (John 8) or one of the prostitutes to whom Jesus extended a second chance? What kind of encounter do you imagine between Jesus and this woman that led up to this dramatic story?

2. The woman appeared at Simon's house for a purpose. Why was she weeping? Why did she anoint Jesus' feet with perfume?

3. What is it about the woman's behavior you find most extravagant? The cost of the perfume? The fact that she poured it on Jesus' feet? The intimacy of her actions (wiping his feet with her hair)? Or the fact that all this was done in full view of a stunned and incredulous audience?

4. Do you imagine that the woman herself, in time, might have been embarrassed about that evening? Would she have wished she had chosen a more private moment? Would she, eventually, be shocked by her own brazenness?

5. The parable Jesus tells (verses 41-42) gives us some hints about the woman's motives for crashing Simon's party. Identify each of the characters in the parable. Who is the money-lender? The one who owed much? The one who owed little? What does the punch line of the parable (verses 42-43) tell us about the motives of this woman?

6. The woman had lived a "sinful life" (verse 37). Simon was an upright Pharisee. But which of them had, at that moment, a consuming passion for God? Is Jesus actually teaching that it's better to be a badly failed person who realizes how much forgiveness God has extended than to be a really good person who feels no need for forgiveness?

7. Jesus' conclusion (see verse 47) seems to imply that love is the *condition* for forgiveness rather than the *result* of it—that love leads to forgiveness rather than the other way around. Does that conclusion contradict the point of the parable Jesus just told? What was Jesus really saying here?

APPLICATION:

1. Who are you most like—the woman or the Pharisee?

- In terms of your past—badly failed or morally upright?
- In terms of your experience of forgiveness—astounded or nonchalant?
- In terms of your gratitude—extravagant or moderate?

2. Do you consider yourself to have been forgiven "little" or "much"? Are there any of us who, in reality, have little to be forgiven? Isn't it only when we compare ourselves to each other (rather than to God) that we can nurture the illusion God has little to forgive in us?

3. Would you agree that the root of a "great love" for God is the experience of a "great forgiveness"? If so, how can we become more amazed by God's grace to love him more? Can you come up with some specific ways to recognize more fully what God has done for you?

4. "I want to be extravagant in my expressions of gratitude to God even if, on occasion, I make a fool of myself doing it." Would you agree with that statement?

COOL DOWN:

In the coming weeks, you'll have an opportunity to do something extravagant to show God your gratitude. Perhaps it will involve giving money or telling your story or serving someone "above and beyond the call of duty." Go around the group and identify some possibilities for being extravagant with God. Encourage each member to make a commitment—to look expectantly for that opportunity, to take the opportunity eagerly, to disregard what others might think, and to refuse to feel embarrassed about doing something a little extreme out of a passion for God. We could use a few more extremists like this woman.

LIVING IT OUT

A hunger for righteousness is an acquired taste. Unlike sexual urges or the craving for food, an appetite for holy things must be developed. It doesn't come naturally.

So how do we develop a taste for righteousness? Psychologists tell us that to develop healthy addictions or to train our passions, we think our way into acting, and then act our way into feeling.

For example, the habit of exercise begins with an awareness of the benefits of exercise and a *decision* to do something active, whether you feel like it or not. That intention must be followed by specific, regular *behavior*—behavior driven by what you know is best rather than what feels best at the moment. Eventually, a feeling for exercise (an addiction to movement) results.

What if the same is true of righteousness? You can't command yourself to be passionate about right living and the things of God. But you can make decisions

and take action. So here are three steps you might want to try as you develop a taste for righteousness.

First, use your head. On a daily basis, consider how much God loves you, how much he has forgiven you, how much he has blessed you. (Gratitude is a pretty powerful motive for righteous behavior.) Choose some specific goals to work on (regular church attendance, a particular sin you need to overcome, a holy habit you'd like to develop), and then make intentional commitments to act on those goals, whether you feel like it or not. Write out your goals and intentions and tape them to your bathroom mirror as a reminder (that mirror is getting pretty full by now!).

Second, act better than you feel. Let your head do the driving for a while rather than your heart. It will help if your goals are specific, if success or failure in attaining them is obvious, and if you accomplish them one day at a time. Going to church every

Sunday is a specific goal. You can easily tell whether you went or not. And you're not making a commitment for the rest of your life—just for *this* Sunday. Daily Bible reading, a regular prayer life, working on a particular sin— each involves righteous behavior that is specific, measurable, and doable today. Pick some holy habit and then act to incorporate it into your life.

Finally, leave the passion to God. Trust that he'll honor your attempts to please him with the gift of a passion for holiness. Look for ways God is shaping your appetites. Notice when vice loses some of its appeal. Be aware when "ought to" becomes "want to." Recognize God's work in your life and give him the glory for it.

The following prayer might be helpful as you learn to hunger for righteousness.

Father,
I don't hunger for you as I should.
So many other appetites, so

*many other passions, compete
with you in my heart. Forgive me,
Father, when I let petty passions
overwhelm my longing for you.
I'm ashamed when that happens.*

*Lord, I want to want you. I
hunger to be hungry for you.
Teach me your ways. Show me
your will. Instruct me in the path I
should walk. Grant me the
strength and the discipline to live
better than I feel, to follow you
even when I would rather do
something else. Let me learn
meekness—to say, "Not my will,
but yours be done."*

*But then, Father, grant me the
gift of passion. Take my weak
intentions and feeble efforts and
transform them into a consuming
passion for you. Fill me with a
zeal for you that captures my
heart and directs my life. Let my
gratitude for what you have done
for me fuel a burning desire to
live for you.*

*I love you, Father. Help me to
live like it. Amen.*

IN A WORD

Hungering for righteousness is the
willingness to say (and mean), **"I
want to do what is right."** The
emphasis here is squarely on the
word "want." This hunger is the
mature stage of meekness—it is
the transformation of "ought to"
into a consuming "want to."

Have MERCY

There is but one love of Jesus as there is but one person in the poor—Jesus.... [With] undivided love we surrender ourselves totally to him in the person who takes his place.
—MOTHER TERESA

According to tradition, the first Christian hermit was Paul of Thebes. Fleeing from persecution around A.D. 250, this disciple took off into the deserts of Egypt, living out the remainder of his life in poverty and solitude. Now there was a man who was serious about discipleship!

Or consider St. Simeon Stylites in the fifth century. Disgusted with the casual Christianity of his contemporaries, Simeon erected a fifty-foot-high pole, built a small platform at the top, and devoted himself to prayer and fasting for the next thirty-five years. He finally died of malnutrition and exposure. Now there was a man who took discipleship seriously!

Have you ever heard of the Carthusian monks? This monastic order, founded in the eleventh century, was formed by a band of men who desired to withdraw from the world (and less-dedicated Christians) in order to fast, pray, and study. Each monk confined himself to a separate cell and maintained a vow of absolute silence. Life for these monks involved physical hardship, social isolation, and spiritual discipline. Now those were people who took discipleship seriously!

> **THE SINGING MONKS**
>
> In the spring of 1994, the monks of Santo Domingo de Silos in northern Spain released *Chant*—a recording of medieval Gregorian chants. The album became an instant success, selling 6 million copies worldwide and grossing more than $50 million. It ascended to #3 on the pop music charts, lodging next to hits by Snoop Doggy Dogg and Nine Inch Nails. Commented the monks: "It's a miracle."
>
> **—Time Magazine**

Or were they?

Something about religion tempts Christians to conclude that the ultimate expression of religious devotion is *vertical*, involving the way we relate to God. From this viewpoint, prayer, study, meditation, worship, and fasting are the holiest skills of religious life. Some seem to think that a disciple is closer to God in his closet than in the press and bustle of daily life. In fact, such people would contend that our interactions with others get in the way of religious pursuits. Someone with this mindset might say, "Serious disciples should minimize such distractions in order to focus more fully on God."

WHAT GOES UP
MUST COME DOWN

Of course, nothing could be further from the truth. Jesus expressed his love for God by entering a world of sinners and suffering, not by remaining in heaven for undistracted devotion to his Father.

> "Blessed are the merciful, for they will be shown mercy."[1]

But as we come to the mid-point of the Beatitudes, all of us are tempted to think like hermits. The first four Beatitudes constitute a long, arduous climb away from ourselves and toward God. Step after laborious step—from poverty to mourning to meekness to hungering and thirsting—we climb Discipleship Mountain into the presence of our Lord. With each stage, we leave self a little farther behind and step that much closer into the realm of the Spirit.

Finally, with hungering and thirsting, we arrive at the pinnacle of spiritual experience. We encounter the presence of God in our lives like never before. We stand on the mountaintop, panting for God, in love with the things he loves.

It's precisely here that we're tempted to define discipleship as life on the mountaintop with God. Like Peter at the Transfiguration (Matthew 17:1-5), we want to build a shelter and stay.

FEAR OF THE PLAIN

Fear of falling down is called "climacophobia."
Fear of crows is known as "ochlophobia."
Fear of strangers is "xenophobia."
And fear of peanut butter sticking to the roof of your mouth is called "arachibutyrophobia."

We enjoy the luxury of an undistracted focus upon the holy. It's wonderful to bask in the presence of God without the bother of other people.

But, if we're honest, it isn't just the appeal of the mountaintop that tempts us to become hermits. It's fear of the plain. It's so much better "up here" than "down there" in the valley of daily life. Down there are people who press and make demands, the sick and the sinful. Down there are difficult people, hard-hearted and spiritually blind. Down there is where the mundane threatens to overwhelm our experience of the transcendent.

And we pray, "It's good for us to be *here*, Lord. Let's stay for a bit—on the mountaintop and far from the madding crowd."

No sooner do those words spill out of us, however, than Jesus points us back down the slope to the plain of ordinary existence. He refuses to let his disciples build shelters up in the clouds. "Your journey is only half done," Jesus tells us. "The true measure of a disciple is not whether you can make it into the presence of God, but whether you can take God's presence back down to the marketplace and the home and the church. It's good for you to be here, but it's not good enough. Disciples don't live *up here.* They live *down there.*"

Had Jesus stopped with "hungering and thirsting for righteousness," serious disciples would be justified in taking off for the desert or secluding themselves in private cells. You don't need anyone else to experience poverty of spirit. You don't require an audience of your peers to mourn. Meekness can be practiced between you and God alone. You can hunger for righteousness in solitude.

But there are eight Beatitudes, not four. Right in the middle of these instructions about discipleship, Jesus changes direction. He doesn't linger long on the mountaintop. With barely a pause, he turns back down the mountain to the messy, noisy, insistent world of people in need.

Any mountain climber will tell you that the most dangerous part of a climb is the descent. More mountaineers make fatal mistakes on the way down than on the way up. The same is true of discipleship. Ascending to the presence of God is the relatively safe part of following Jesus. It's falling off the mountain back into normal life that poses the greatest danger.

So be careful. We're about to make our way back down.

KEEPING THE "ME" IN MERCY
We hand folks over to God's mercy and show none ourselves.
—GEORGE ELIOT

Frankly, we're not all that eager to follow Jesus as he starts down the mountain. We'd prefer to define discipleship as a haven from the troubles of life, an escape from the cold and ugly world. Behind the comforting walls of faith we'd flee, locking the gate behind us and pulling up the drawbridge. We seek isolation, not engagement — insulation from the world's pain, not encounter. We expect our faith to keep us above the fray, to protect us personally from suffering and need, and buffer us emotionally from the anguish of others.

So when we hear Jesus pronounce a blessing on the merciful, we're quick to interpret mercy in a way that doesn't require us to get our hands dirty. We reduce mercy to something manageable, something safe. To accomplish our resistance to this Beatitude, we employ two schemes.

First, we find a way to make mercy synonymous with forgiveness.

Blessed are those who forgive others, for they will be forgiven.

We convince ourselves that Jesus

FATAL DISASTERS
From 1921 to 1996, 144 people lost their lives attempting to climb Mt. Everest. Twelve of these were killed in one month during the spring of 1996 — all of them in the act of *descending* the mountain!
—Into Thin Air

is talking about our obligation to pardon any offenses committed against us. Jesus *does* want us to be forgiving. He *does* expect us to excuse whatever wrongs others do to us. He says as much later in the Sermon on the Mount:

For if you forgive men when they sin against you, your heavenly Father will also forgive you.[2]

But limiting mercy to forgiveness is too neat. That kind of mercy requires only enough contact with others to occasion offense. It's a reactive mercy, called into play when someone blunders into us. As good Christians, we'll turn the other cheek when people slap us in the face. But such mercy extends only as far as our own fragile egos. It still permits us to remain aloof, doling out absolution when necessary and keeping to ourselves otherwise.

Mercy is bigger than forgiveness and requires more than a willingness to pardon the stupidities of others. Forgiveness is but one of its many fruits. When Jesus says, "Blessed are the merciful," he commends disciples who are generous with others' faults. But the generosity Jesus recommends goes much further.

In the Gospels, when blind men begged Jesus to "have mercy,"[3] they were asking not for pardon but for pity. When a Gentile woman pleaded for mercy on behalf of her sick daughter[4] or a father requested mercy for his epileptic son,[5] these parents were appealing for compassion, not absolution. Suffering people cried "Mercy!" to Jesus throughout his ministry. They pushed their way into his crowded agenda to say, "Look at me! See my condition. Be moved by my plight. Do something to relieve my suffering." What they wanted from Jesus at such moments wasn't forgiveness of sin but his attention and gracious response.

Mercy is compassion. It's a vulnerability of heart to the needs of others. It's a willingness to pause from our own busy agendas and self-involved pursuits to hear the cries of people, be moved by those cries, and act in compassion. Mercy is a willingness to identify with the suffering of others, to step into the shoes of hurting people and associate with their plight. Mercy is having the courage to step down from the mountaintop and out of ourselves to be confronted by the predicaments of hurting humanity. Mercy is the state of mind and the condition of heart that permits us to be moved by the desperate souls who disturb our comfortable lives with their insistent cries for help.

MERCY IS A VERB

What value has compassion that does not take its object in its arms?

—ANTOINE DE SAINT-EXUPÉRY

This leads us to the second scheme we employ to evade this Beatitude. If first we tried to limit mercy to forgiveness

> **HEARTS IN GOOD CONDITION**
> The average heart beats 100,000 times each day. That's about 3 billion beats in an average lifetime.
> — American Heart Association

(ignoring Christ's call to compassion), next we attempt to limit mercy to a warm feeling (ignoring Christ's call to action). Too often and for too long, disciples of Jesus have excused their lack of direct involvement with needy people by taking refuge in pious references to the depth of their compassionate feelings. We seem to imagine that sympathetic sentiments are a substitute for healing actions.

For years, I've carried a card that expresses this lie well.

Your story has touched my heart. Never before have I been so moved by the suffering of another human being. You have my deepest and sincerest sympathies. Please accept this card as an expression of my heartfelt sorrow for your plight.

Try giving that card to a woman who is weeping over her rebellious daughter or a man who is contemplating suicide. Try whipping it out when someone has lost everything in a natural disaster or needs your help struggling through a crisis of character. It's laughable to even contemplate offering such words in the place of personal involvement. It's tragic that this is precisely what we often do.

James, the brother of Jesus, noted the same tendency to prefer words over actions in disciples of his own day.

Suppose a brother or sister is without clothes and daily food. If one of you says to him, "Go, I wish you well; keep warm and well fed," but does nothing about his physical needs, what good is it?[6]

Mercy is more than being "moved with compassion"—unless you put the emphasis on the word "moved." Mercy will not allow us to take refuge in tender feelings and empty phrases. It may begin as a feeling, but it quickly moves forth in tangible behaviors. Mercy doesn't describe an emotion so much as an activity.

Like faith, mercy apart from works is dead.

Whenever people cried out to Jesus for mercy, Jesus gave them more than his pity—he *did* something about their need. Sometimes, his compassion resulted in healing. On other occasions, compassion blossomed into forgiveness or food or teaching.[7] Ultimately, the greatest fruit of mercy in the life of Jesus was the Cross. Mercy resulted in action where Jesus was concerned. Where there is no compassionate activity, there has been no true mercy.

This kind of tender and active mercy can't be practiced from the mountaintop. It demands a full immersion into the lives of other people. It requires that we be close enough to suffering people to hear their groans and feel their troubles. It obligates us to be bothered about people in pain. It insists we extend ourselves to help.

Do you need me to draw you a picture of mercy? Let Jesus.

A PORTRAIT OF MERCY

"A man was going down from Jerusalem to Jericho,

when he fell into the hands of robbers. They stripped him of his clothes, beat him and went away, leaving him half dead. A priest happened to be going down the same road, and when he saw the man, he passed by on the other side. So too, a Levite, when he came to the place and saw him, passed by on the other side. But a Samaritan, as he traveled, came where the man was; and when he saw him, he took pity on him. He went to him and bandaged his wounds, pouring on oil and wine. Then he put the man on his own donkey, took him to an inn and took care of him. The next day he took out two silver coins and gave them to the innkeeper. 'Look after him,' he said, 'and when I return, I will reimburse you for any extra expense you may have.'

"Which of these three do you think was a neighbor to the man who fell into the hands of robbers?"

The expert in the law replied, *"The one who had mercy on him."*

Jesus told him, "Go and do likewise." [8]

In this story, we meet four people on the road from Jerusalem to Jericho.

The first is a man in crisis. We don't know his name or his station in life. We don't know whether he was careless or simply in the wrong place at the wrong time. All we know is that he "fell into the hands of robbers." He lay in a ditch at the side of the road— naked, bleeding, and half dead.

We know a little more about the three other travelers we meet in this story—something about their race and occupations. Most of all, we know they had to decide what to do with the man in the ditch. He's a stranger. He's a mess. Dealing with him would take time and effort and money. At the least, it would be inconvenient to help this victim.

Two of the travelers decide

BLEEDING VICTIMS

In 1994, it's estimated that more than 9 million Americans were victims of assault. The most likely place to be murdered, mugged, or beaten? Washington, D.C.

—FBI: Uniform Crime Reports

not to involve themselves. In that moment of decision, they opt for apathy instead of mercy. Only the last traveler, a Samaritan, stops to help. In the end, only he "had mercy."

Jesus told this story because a religious expert, who was smart enough to know that "loving your neighbor" is central to the Law, didn't understand what those words meant. Jesus wanted to make the point that "loving your neighbor" means "being merciful to anyone who is in need." To do that, he told the story of the good Samaritan. Don't be sidetracked, however, by the road or the robbers or the characters we meet in this story. The important point is the portrait of mercy Jesus paints. With this story, Jesus teaches what mercy is all about. He points out three things that separate those who show mercy and those who don't.

"Mercy requires eyes that see," Jesus says first. All three

of the travelers saw the fellow in the ditch. The priest saw (verse 31), the Levite saw (verse 32), and the Samaritan saw (verse 33). But there is seeing and there is *seeing!* The priest and Levite saw and looked quickly away. They saw, but pretended they had not. The Samaritan, on the other hand, refused to avert his gaze. He saw a *man* in the ditch, not a messy inconvenience. Perhaps he even saw himself in that man's place, hurting and in need of help. The beginning of mercy is having eyes that can stand to look upon the suffering of other people — eyes that look and do not look away.

"Mercy," says Jesus, "also requires a heart that pities." All three of these travelers were "moved" by what they saw. The priest and Levite were moved — to the other side of the road. They were repulsed by this victim. No spark of compassion was ignited in their hearts. The Samaritan, in contrast, was moved with "pity" (verse 33). Where the

feelings of the priest and Levite drove them away from the ditch to "the other side," the Samaritan was drawn by his feelings to the man. His heart went out first, prompting his feet to follow. Mercy is more than seeing others' pain and blood and need. Open eyes must be connected to a heart that feels compassion.

"Mercy requires hands that act," Jesus concludes. The priest and Levite had *feet* that acted. They quickened their pace and hurried past this bloodied stranger. But only the Samaritan was willing to dirty his hands in order to show mercy. His hands bandaged the wounded man, poured wine and oil on his injuries, and steadied him on the donkey. Samaritan hands carried this victim into a rented room, fed him broth, and placed cool cloths on his brow. Samaritan hands reached into a purse for money and sealed a deal with the innkeeper. To eyes that notice and a heart that pities must be added hands that

act — if mercy is to happen.

"Which of these three was a neighbor?" Jesus asked the expert. "The one who had mercy on him," came the reply. The one who saw and would not look away. The one whose heart was moved with compassion. The one who set his hands to relieving another's pain.

The world and suffering humanity create the agenda for those who have eyes for human misery, ears for the stories of oppression, and hearts to respond to the distress of our human family.
—Cardinal Basil Hume

NEIGHBOR
The neighbor has become a stock character in sitcoms. While not lead roles, TV neighbors can become as famous as the stars of our favorite shows. Famous neighbors:
Fred and Ethel — "I Love Lucy"
Wilson — "Home Improvement"
Kramer — "Seinfeld"

EVADING MERCY
It's interesting that the religious people in this story are the ones who can't muster any mercy. It takes a Samaritan — someone disliked by the Jews of Jesus' day and seen as a religious half-breed — to demonstrate this quality for us. We assume that

these two clergymen "passed by on the other side" because they were evil, hard-hearted, and calloused. They play to our prejudices about Jewish religious leaders in those days—Pharisees, chief priests, Sadduccees, and the like. The whole lot of them are viewed as corrupt, ungodly, and hypocritical by modern readers of the New Testament.

Perhaps these two *were* scoundrels. There's never been any shortage of ministerial rogues. But there may be another explanation for their behavior. It doesn't have the advantage of appealing to our prejudices. And it has the distinct disadvantage of touching a sensitive spot in ourselves. But it does commend itself for one reason—it's the most plausible explanation I can think of for why they (and we) avoid the mandate for mercy.

When we meet the priest and the Levite in this story, they're traveling from Jerusalem to Jericho[9]—probably on their way from conducting their respective duties at the temple to resuming their duties at home. Men in their positions played an important role in the affairs of Israel. Priests made sacrifices and conducted the worship in the temple, and Levites assisted them with other tasks required to keep the temple running. Priests and Levites were prominent members of their community, with responsibilities in the synagogue and in local government. Having just completed their business on the mountain of God, now they're rushing home to take care of the "holy things" awaiting them there.

There on the road, caught between church and home, these two betray an attitude about religion many Christians share. They exhibit the same tendency to define religion *vertically* that we noted in ourselves. The real business of religion is connected with the rituals, routines, and rhythms of the temple and the synagogue. Piety and obedience consist of keeping the laws, poring over sacred texts, and discharging ecclesiastic responsibilities. "Spirituality" is about worship and daily prayers and tithing and fasting. Religion has little to do with a wounded man on the side of the road.

I doubt it ever occurred to the priest and the Levite that leaving a man in the ditch might reflect badly on their devotion to God.

On another day—less preoccupied with the sermon they just heard, with more time on their hands because services had not run long—the priest and Levite might have stopped to lend a hand. If they didn't have to run right home to hold evening services at the synagogue, lead a devotional for the family, and visit a sick parishioner, they might have taken time for mercy. But these two have just been to the mountaintop! They're still engrossed with the high and the holy. They have critical theological business to attend to back home. They can't afford to be distracted from the service of God by an inconvenient sufferer.

If there's any substance to

the above conjectures, the priest and Levite "pass by on the other side" less because they're cruel and more because they just don't see mercy as a central part of their walk with God. They've defined worship as praising God, not wiping blood from a stranger. They've managed to move mercy to the periphery of religious life. They've made mercy a luxury in which—given time and inclination—religious people should indulge on occasion. But not *this* time. Not now.

It's easy to dismiss the priest and Levite as merely evil men, to reduce them to caricatures rather than treat them as people with whom we should identify—religious folk who struggle as we do. Because *we* are not evil, they have nothing to teach us. But if ever we allow the possibility that they failed to show mercy for the same reasons we do, that they excused themselves from helping with the same justifications we employ, then, suddenly, we find ourselves wondering why we're

so much like the priest and Levite when it's the Samaritan who is the hero of this story.

THE LEVITE IN ALL OF US

Every day of our lives, you and I are confronted with bleeding people—people Satan has beaten and stripped and left for dead on the side of the road. Perhaps it's a neighbor who interrupts your evening to talk about marriage problems. Maybe it's a friend who keeps crawling inside a bottle and calling you to find the way out. Perhaps it's that brother who comes forward at church for prayers and financial assistance. It could even be a stranger stranded on the side of the road, in need of a meal and a place to stay for the night.

There are people all around us in crisis, in pain, in need. They barge into our consciousness uninvited, assaulting our privacy and disturbing our peace. They make our telephones jangle, asking that we stop what we're doing to attend to their problems. They confront us on the streets, at

the workplace, in the foyer at church crying, "Mercy! Look at me! See my condition. Be moved by my plight. Help relieve my suffering!"

Like the priest, Levite, and Samaritan, we must decide what to do with people in the ditch. Will we see them? Will our hearts be moved to pity? Will our hands reach out to help? All too often, the hard answer to that question is "no."

It's not that we're evil and hardhearted, uncaring and apathetic toward hurting people. None of us are *Levites*, thank goodness! We've just managed to move mercy to the periphery of discipleship. We don't consider random acts of kindness to be an essential part of Christian living. We have more important things to do than stop and lend a hand.

We've defined the real business of discipleship as something that takes place up on the mountaintop, at the Holy of Holies, where we can focus fully on our

> ### SPEAKING OF CRAWLING INSIDE A BOTTLE . . .
> About 9 percent of American adults can be classified as "alcohol dependent." More than a half million of them will seek treatment for alcohol addiction each year. Researchers estimate that more than 50 percent will fall off the recovery wagon some time in the first three months of their treatment.
> —National Institute of Health

Father. We've understood piety and obedience in terms of holding up moral standards, quoting Bible texts, and going to church. For many of us, "spirituality" concerns dynamic worship periods and fervent prayers and supporting missionaries. But the essence of discipleship has little to do with wounded people on the side of the road.

So consumed are we by the "real" business of discipleship, we simply can't afford to be distracted by yet another stranger with still another need. We're so busy with kingdom stuff, we just don't have the time or energy to pick up broken people. We're so filled with passion for spiritual things, there's little compassion left to spend on the needy and the wounded and the lost.

The very idea that mercy is at the core of kingdom business, that discipleship divorced from mercy is dead, never occurs to us. We've managed to make mercy a luxury that, given time and inclination, disciples should indulge on occasion. But not *this* time. Not now.

THE LIMITS OF MERCY

By compassion we make others' misery our own, and so, by relieving them, we relieve ourselves also.

—SIR THOMAS BROWNE

Failing to limit mercy to forgiveness, unsuccessful at reducing mercy to a sentiment, our final scheme to evade mercy involves demoting it on the list of a disciple's spiritual priorities. Surely there are some things more important than mercy!

We want to hear Jesus say to the paralytic lowered through the roof of a house for healing,[10] "Not now! Can't you see I'm in the middle of preaching about the kingdom of heaven?"

We want Jesus to say to the woman who touched his garment in the crowd,[11] "Look! I'm on my way to raise a dead girl back to life. You'll just have to bleed quietly until I can get to you. Please wait your turn!"

We want Jesus to tell the woman who crashed the party at Simon the Pharisee's house (weeping at his feet and begging forgiveness),[12] "This is not a convenient time, lady! And please don't touch me like that. Everyone is watching!"

We want Jesus to tell the man with the shriveled hand who stood up in the synagogue one Sabbath and asked to be healed,[13] "Can't we talk later? If I heal you on the Sabbath, these Pharisees will start plotting to kill me. What kind of Messiah would I be if I jeopardized my ministry to take care of one crippled man?"

And most of all, we want Jesus to tell that thief on the cross, "Buddy, I'm sorry. But right now I happen to be dying for the sins of the world. I just don't have the time to talk to you about paradise. Where were you three years ago? I would have been glad to talk to you then. But nooooo! You were out knocking people over the head and stealing their money. You made your own cross, friend. Now hang on it!"

We want Jesus to say those things because those are the things we say (or at least think) to excuse ourselves from the requirement for mercy. We want Jesus to suggest there are other things more important to the kingdom than being merciful. We want to see in Jesus an example of times when mercy takes a back seat to other religious priorities. We hope Jesus will pass a few people by on the side of the road as he hurries on to address the central issues of religious life.

But he never does. Jesus is never so focused on God that he's blind to hurting people. He's never so busy doing kingdom work that he can't stop to bind up the wounded and comfort the hurting and befriend the lonely. Throughout his ministry, Jesus was careless with mercy. He gave it away, sometimes even *threw* it away. He spread mercy around as if there were no limits. He shoveled it out by the bucketful. His ear was always tuned to the despairing cry. His eye was ever vigilant for the unfortunate and the damaged.

When asked to define his mission on earth, Jesus answered in terms of mercy: "[God] has anointed me to preach good news to the poor.

He has sent me to proclaim freedom for the prisoners and recovery of sight for the blind, to release the oppressed."[14] When asked to name the greatest commandment, he wouldn't stop until he'd spoken of mercy: "Love your neighbor as yourself."[15] When castigating the religious leaders of his time for being consumed with the tiny details and neglecting the "more important matters of the law," Jesus listed mercy as one of the three things religious people can't afford to ignore.[16]

For Jesus, mercy isn't something to be tacked on to the end of religious devotions. Mercy isn't an option that godly people get around to when other work is done. Far from being at the periphery of faith, mercy is at the core of discipleship for Jesus.

I think that's why he lists mercy right after the hunger for righteousness. He wants us to understand that discipleship doesn't stop with a passion for God. Disciples who are "so heavenly minded they are no

earthly good" aren't much good to Jesus. He wants us to know that when we have climbed the mountain into the presence of God, we'll be given three gifts: eyes to see hurting people, hearts that can be moved to pity, and hands that will reach to help. Only those who are willing to carry those gifts "down there" and put them to use can be disciples of Jesus.

OUT OF THE WARMTH AND INTO THE COLD

O Lord, baptise our hearts into a sense of the conditions and need of all men.

—George Fox

I was first initiated into the world of hot rocks and cedar as a teenager. It was the Finnish who invented the sauna. They claim it's invigorating to bake in a small, dark oven to the point of heat exhaustion and then immerse yourself in a pool of ice-cold water. As I recall, I didn't mind the baking part. It was the baptism I objected to. Several adults were required to

SAUNA
Correctly pronounced "sow (rhymes with wow) nah," this is the only Finnish word imported into the English language. Currently there are 5 million people in Finland, and about 1.7 million saunas.
— www.saunasite.com

pry my fevered fingers from the seat of the sauna, free my blistered feet from their wedged position against the door frame, and throw me bodily into a pool of water that no self-respecting penguin would have entered.

What Jesus does with us when he speaks of mercy is uncomfortably analogous. The first four Beatitudes demand that we spend time in the closet with God—a focused period of quiet meditation and personal introspection. It's "hot" in that closet, as though God were baking himself a disciple. Yet we learn to enjoy that environment. There's something relaxing about warming ourselves in the presence of God and sweating out a lifetime of impurity.

But no sooner do we acclimate to the closet than Jesus flings open the door and points to the icy waterworld outside. With his blessing on the merciful, Jesus invites us to immerse ourselves bodily in the cold realities of human existence. He never intended religion to be something we practice in the sauna (or on the mountaintop). He speaks these final Beatitudes so that we can be different *from* the world even as we live *in* the world.

Not that we go willingly, of course. We require dragging. Jesus must pry our fingers from the pews. He must dislodge the feet we have wedged under the routines and rituals of normal religious life. He must loosen the death grip we have on the private and the personal. Though he would prefer that we go willingly out into the cold, most often he has to hurl us bodily into the frigid pool of the world's pain. It's freezing out there. There's sin and suffering out there. There are endless and urgent needs out among our fellows.

So we fight Jesus tooth and nail. "It's good for us to be *here*. Don't make us go out *there!*" But Jesus just smiles and shows us the nail prints in his hands.

He points to the world and says that *out there* is where religion becomes useful and disciples do their best work.

Ice-cold water after a red-hot sauna is, in fact, incredibly exhilarating. I never realized how alive such a plunge could make you feel. Oh, people told me I'd enjoy the experience. They even went first and led by example. But I didn't really believe them. Not until that first breathtaking dip of my own!

Mercy is much the same. Yes, it's risky. Certainly, it takes us out of our comfort zones. Yet it's incredibly stimulating. But you have to experience it. Wade out into the lives of hurting, needy people and you'll be amazed how refreshed, how alive, such contact can make you feel.

Others can tell you about it. They can dive in and yell that the water is fine. But you won't believe them. Not until you're willing to jump in and try it yourself.

Go on. Try it. You'll like it.

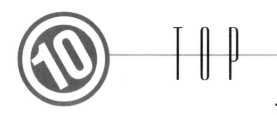

TOP TEN . . .

TOP TEN DANGERS OF TRYING TO BE MERCIFUL

10. Your favorite song, "Here's a quarter, call someone who cares," now seems strangely inappropriate.

9. The claim that your entire life is a "not-for-profit" ministry prompts an IRS audit.

8. You might die in horrible agony from wounds sustained in battle. No, wait! That's a danger of being merc—enary.

7. You must endure dirty looks from bums at the Plasma Center when you refuse to take money for your blood donation.

6. You're often rear-ended by motorists who fail to notice your "I brake for victims in the ditch" bumper sticker.

5. You suddenly develop an abdominal pouch in which you nurse your young. No, wait! That's a danger of being merc—upial.

4. You find yourself sounding more and more like Bill Clinton. ("I feel your pain!")

3. Your boss fires you because he doesn't believe that cockamamie story about extra hotel room expenses.

2. You're forced to drive luxurious German automobiles with bad gas mileage and expensive repair bills. No, wait! That's the danger of owning a Merc—edes.

And the **#1** danger of trying to become merciful:

Elders reprimand you for titling your sermon on the good Samaritan:

"Get Down Off Your Ass and Help Somebody!"

THE STORY OF . . .

Mother Teresa

THE SISTER OF MERCY

In the fall of 1997, a withered, wizened, wisp of a woman died. That, in itself, is unremarkable. It happens all the time. Only this time, the whole world paused to mourn. For the woman was Mother Teresa. And her fame was rooted—not in her beauty, power, or wealth—but in a lifetime devoted to mercy.

Born in Albania to a prosperous building contractor, she determined early on to devote herself to the poor. At eighteen, she joined the Sisters of Loretto, a community of nuns who ran schools in India. For the next two decades, she taught geography at a convent school in Calcutta. Always just outside her window, however, was a flowing river of human misery—a river unaffected by geography lessons delivered to middle-class children.

In 1946, Teresa "heard the call to give up all and follow [Jesus] to the slums." For the next four years, she made repeated requests to the Pope to be released from her work at the convent to pursue a mission of mercy. In 1950, the Pope "uncloistered" Teresa, permitting her to work independently. She set out into Calcutta's streets, without money or a plan, knowing only that she was to minister to the "unwanted, unloved, and uncared for."

She began teaching slum children to read and write, using vacant lots for classrooms and mud puddles for blackboards. It was they who named her "Mother Teresa"—a term of affection later adopted by the world.

One day, however, she came upon a woman "half-eaten by maggots and rats" lying in the street. Teresa sat with her, stroking her head and praying, until the woman died. A new vocation was born. She understood that God was calling her to extend his mercy to the most miserable and destitute and dying.

Her first "Home for the Destitute and Dying" was a hostel that had once served pilgrims to the Temple of Kali—the Hindu goddess of death and destruction. Teresa and a few followers began scooping up the dying from the city's gutters and taking them to the Home where they could die in peace. One of the sect of Kali's priests knocked on their door. Afflicted with leprosy, the man had been expelled from the temple and turned out into the streets to die. Teresa gave him a dying place.

During the next forty-five years, Mother Teresa continued to expand her ministry of mercy. The Missionary Sisters of Charity attracted novices from all over the world. In addition to the three traditional vows of poverty, chastity, and obedience, those who would join Mother Teresa were required to take a vow of "wholehearted free service to the poorest of the poor." Today, they number more than 4,500 with 550 centers in 126 countries. They serve not only the poor, but also those dying of AIDS, battered women, and drug addicts.

What I find most impressive about Mother Teresa, however, was not her selfless service, but the reason she gave herself to the poor. Mother Teresa saw "Christ in his distressing disguise" in every person she met. Ann Petrie, who directed a 1986 film about Mother Teresa, said of her:

Rather than regarding the poor as a problem, she saw every human being, no matter how wretched, as an opportunity to do something for Jesus.

In a dying woman, Mother Teresa saw Jesus and an opportunity to serve him. In a leper or an AIDS victim or a drug addict, she saw some glimmer of Jesus and a chance to offer him comfort. Her ministry was not just to the sick and poor and dying—it was to the Christ she saw in each of them. Some might say she spent her life ministering to nobodies. She would respond that, whatever she did for the nobodies, she was doing for her Lord.

At the death of this noble woman, words of admiration and respect poured in from all over the world. Of course, it's easier to admire mercy than to practice it. Queen Elizabeth praised Mother Teresa's "untiring devotion to the poor and destitute of all religions"—but she did it in a press statement released from her castle. President Clinton called Mother Teresa "one of the giants of our time"—but he paused in the middle of a game of golf to do so. The Pope reacted strongly—"Her death touched his heart very deeply," a Vatican spokesman reported for the Pontiff who was vacationing at his summer residence.

But before you look down on these people for their palaces and privileges in contrast to the renounced life of Mother Teresa, you might want to examine yourself. Mercy is always inconvenient. It will always cost you something, demand some sacrifice, require some self-denial. Mother Teresa gave up everything for the sake of mercy. What are you willing to give up for the sake of others? Between the complete renunciation of Mother Teresa and the grasping self-absorption of so many in our world, there's a great deal of room for the rest of us to say "no" to ourselves and "yes" to the needs of those around us.

Or better put, there are countless opportunities for Christians to say "no" to ourselves and "yes" to our Lord—who hides himself in the suffering people we encounter every day.[17]

THINKING IT THROUGH

MONDAY

Reading the Bible, it doesn't take long to discover people who thought of religion as an entirely vertical business. Cain was upset that his sacrifice was rejected but not all that disturbed about killing his brother. David could write beautiful psalms but murder the husband of a woman he wanted. Read the following stories and indicate how these people failed to respect the horizontal aspects of their faith.

- Judges 11:30-40—The story of Jephthah
- Isaiah 1:10-17—The people of Israel
- Mark 12:38-40—The teachers of the Law
- 1 Corinthians 11:17-22, 33-34—The Corinthian Christians
- James 2:14-17—The Jewish Christians
- 1 John 3:11-18—The Christians in Asia Minor

TUESDAY

The Bible never restricts religious activities to the temple or the church building. Compassionate actions, caring for needy people and looking out for the weak and defenseless, have always been a part of the holy life. Read the passages below. What compassionate action is recommended? Who is the beneficiary of that action? Who is called upon to act in compassionate ways?

- Deuteronomy 15:1-11; 24:19-22
- Psalms 82:1-4
- Proverbs 14:31; 19:17; 21:13; 22:9; 28:27
- Matthew 19:21
- Luke 14:12-14
- James 1:27

WEDNESDAY

We took a close look at the parable of the good Samaritan in this chapter. Read the parable again (Luke 10:25-37) and answer the following questions.

1. What did the expert in the Law hope to accomplish by asking the question, "Who is my neighbor?" What do you think he wanted to hear?

2. Jesus responded to this question by telling a story about an interaction between two strangers (not even of the same race or religion). What does that tell us about "neighbor" and about "mercy"?

3. We often excuse ourselves from helping people on the side of the road because of the risks that might be involved. I'm all for prudence and caution. But what this Samaritan did was not without danger. What risks did he run by stopping to help?

4. Note that Jesus doesn't define neighbor by geographical proximity or surface similarities. How does he define neighbor? What does this teach us about the meaning of "love your neighbor as yourself"?

THURSDAY

There are other stories about mercy in the Bible. Read the following passages. Who is being merciful? Who is mercy being shown to? What form does mercy take?

- 1 Kings 17:8-16—Elijah and the widow of Zarephath
- Ruth 2:1-12—Ruth and Boaz
- Jeremiah 38:1-13—Jeremiah and Ebed-Melech
- Acts 3:1-8—Peter and a lame man
- Philemon 1:7-19—Paul, Philemon, and Onesimus

FRIDAY

Jesus always had time for mercy. Not even the most urgent vertical business took precedence over acts of kindness to people in need. As you read the following passages, note: (1) what religious business Jesus was doing, (2) how people in need interrupted him, and (3) how Jesus responded to them.

- Mark 2:1-5
- Mark 5:22-34
- Luke 7:36-50
- Luke 6:6-11
- Luke 23:39-43

What was the most significant lesson you learned in your study this week?

TALKING IT OVER

TEXT: MATTHEW 25:31-46

WARM-UP:
Have you ever treated someone rudely, insincerely, thoughtlessly—only to discover later that he or she was someone to whom you should have paid more attention? Share with the group a time when you virtually ignored a stranger, and then found out he was related to the person you were dating, or was your boss's boss, or was in a position to benefit you in some way.

Often how we treat strangers is determined by our first impressions of them. If we judge them to be rich, beautiful, successful, or influential, we focus our full attention on them. If we see them as poor, failed, flawed, or insignificant, we're likely to look right past them. Do you agree?

We get into trouble when our first impressions are wrong. Or rather, we get into trouble when we accept the notion that some people just don't deserve the attention we're willing to give others.

Well, we're not the only ones. Read Matthew 25:31-46.

DISCUSSION:
Look first at the people who are in "need" in this parable.

1. The "sheep" and the "goats" both came into contact with people who needed their attention and mercy. What kind of needs did those people have? List them.

2. Which category would these people fall into? The successful or the failed? The rich or the poor? The powerful or the pitiful?

3. Honestly now—would we be more likely to pay close attention to these people or look past them because they can do nothing for us?

Note the difference the Son of Man saw between the "sheep" and the "goats."

4. How did the "sheep" respond to needy people? The "goats"?

5. Mercy is the knife the Son of Man used to cut between these two groups. The "blessed" show it; the "cursed" do not. Of all the criteria Jesus could have used to judge people, does it seem strange that he chose mercy? What does this tell us about where mercy falls in God's priorities?

Now for the punch line. Notice that these poor, needy people are not who they appear to be.

6. The "Son of Man" does not say, "*They* were hungry." He says, "*I* was hungry." Read verses 40 and 45 again. Who is Jesus identifying with in this parable?

7. Did either the righteous or the cursed recognize Jesus in the person of the poor? Did they realize who they were dealing with when they showed (or failed to show) mercy?

8. If they had realized that what they did for the needy was "doing" for Jesus, what difference might it have made for each group?

9. What is the final conclusion of the parable? What happens to the "sheep" and the "goats"?

APPLICATION:

1. Can you tell of a time when you acted like the "sheep" in this story? Have you ever acted like the "goats"?

2. Do first impressions make a difference in the way you react to people? Do you find yourself looking past people who don't impress you very much?

3. Have you trained yourself to see Jesus hiding in the person of the needy? What difference would it make for you if you were convinced you were serving Christ himself? Would you be a more merciful person?

4. Starvation and nakedness may not be the greatest needs in your neighborhood. What would you say are the most pressing opportunities to serve the people who live and work around you?

COOL DOWN:

If you were to ask five hundred people whether they'd rather be the "sheep" or the "goats" in this parable, how many would choose "goats"? None? Yet many of those same people will probably be judged as "goats" when the Lord comes again. What we say we want and what we're willing to live out aren't always in harmony.

Go around the group. Have each member pledge to see Christ in others and to be more merciful this week. Close with a prayer asking God to make you the kind of merciful servant to whom Jesus will show mercy.

LIVING IT OUT

In this chapter, we learned that mercy requires eyes that see, a heart that feels, and hands that act. Here are some ideas to help you become more aware of the hurting people around you, more empathetic to their plight, and more active in your efforts to help.

The first step to mercy involves becoming more aware of the needs of those around you. Learning to see people in pain is not as easy as it sounds. Most of us are so busy navel-gazing, it takes a conscious effort to look up and notice the true condition of the people we meet.

It can be done. Perhaps the best way to start is to value the "little mercies." Most of the needs we encounter each day are more subtle than starvation and nakedness. They involve loneliness, grief, despair, lack of purpose. Are you aware of the needs of the people you work with, the folks you worship with, the guy at the gas station or the grocery store? Have you stopped long enough to consider what their struggles might be?

Set aside one day this week as an "others" day. Carry a notebook with you and jot down the names of all the people you have more than passing contact with. (List the names in a column along the left-hand side of the page.) That evening, add a second column (in the center of the page) titled "Need." Were you listening closely enough today to hear a particular struggle each person was facing? Write that struggle beside each name.

Now do some reflecting. If you have a need listed beside every name, your awareness is good—it's your heart or your hands that keep you from showing mercy, not your eyes. If only half the names have needs beside them, you should question whether you're really listening, whether you notice the troubles people face. If few of the names have a need beside them, perhaps you should spend some time in prayer—asking God to heal your blindness to others. You might also spend some time learning to be a better listener.

Once you notice the needs of others, the question becomes, "Do you care?" Pick out two or three people on your list—people you're already concerned about and would like to help. How can you deepen your sense of compassion for their needs?

These three things might help. First, seek to *understand*. Talk to these people. Take them to lunch and listen to what they're experiencing, how their need is affecting them. Hear what life is like from their perspective. Second, *identify* with them. Imagine what it would be like for you to go through a divorce or face a financial crisis or fight bouts of depression. Put yourself in their shoes. Third, *spiritualize* these people. See them as Jesus in disguise. Recognize that Jesus is hurting with them, that easing their pain is easing his.

There. Feel more compassionate? Then what are you going to *do* about it? Seeing hurts and caring about hurts is of little use unless you find a way to help with those hurts. To our open eyes and open hearts, we must now add open hands.

Go back to your list. In a third column (on the right-hand side of the page titled "Help"), write down one thing you could do to show mercy and give comfort to each of these people. Don't make the help impractical ("Pay off

Suzie's $100,000 debt") or unrealistic ("Become Tom's best friend for rest of life"). Put down something tangible and achievable—not something you might do, but something you will do. Think of specific acts of mercy that would be of help to these people. You don't have to fix their lives. You don't have to make everything better. But you can find one simple, useful way to say, "I care about you and I want to help."

The following prayer might help you become a more merciful person.

Father,
I've been so richly blessed. You've given me so much. Every day I enjoy the mercies you pour upon me.
Teach me to be grateful for your mercies, Lord. But teach me also to imitate your mercy as I interact with other people. Help me to have your eyes, so I may see the needs of those around me. Give me your heart, so I might be moved by what I see. And lend me your hands, Lord, so I can know how to serve people in effective and helpful ways.

I don't want to pass by hurting people on my hurried way through life. You paused to lift me up and bind my wounds and heal my pain. Grant me the grace to do the same for others. Amen.

IN A WORD

Mercy is an eagerness to say, **"Let me help you."** It's the capacity to see the pain of others, to feel for people in pain, and to take active measures to alleviate that pain. Mercy does what it can, when it can, for whomever it can.

The REAL THING

When the devil goes to Mass he hides his tail.

—CREOLE PROVERB

urglars don them before holding up banks. Children wear them around the neighborhood, knocking on doors and demanding, "Trick or treat!" They're standard attire for any self-respecting superhero.

Masks have a long history in almost every culture around the world. The earliest masks—carved from wood or shaped of clay or woven from fibers—were intended less to hide the identity of the wearer than to transform it. By putting on a particular mask, ancient performers put on the identities of spirits (in religious rituals) or characters (in plays) or famous people (in historical reenactments).

With time, however, the primary function of masks evolved. No longer did they serve to represent but to obscure. The Lone Ranger's mask was intended to keep his true identity secret. The use of masks at Carnival and Mardi Gras permits participants to carouse anonymously. Members of the Klan wear masks, not as fashion statements, but as concealment.

Concealment is the main idea emphasized by the word mask in modern times. To mask something is to obscure it and keep it hidden. To wear a mask means to put on a disguise,

> ### MORE ON MASKS
> If you want to know more about masks, *The Encyclopedia Britannica* has an excellent article—creatively titled "Masks." Also, John Mack edits a colorful and interesting volume called *Masks and the Art of Expression*.

"Blessed are the pure in heart, for they will see God."[1]

to cover the real face with a false one. Unmasking is something done to spies and frauds— it allows the person behind the façade to be revealed.

Of course, the masks we talk about these days are no longer physical objects you can touch. We're too sophisticated to craft masks out of mud or metal. The disguises worn today are formed from different stuff—deceit, pretense, affectation. Modern masks are manufactured, not by people who are skilled with their hands, but by people who are willing and able to disguise private realities with public fictions.

Would you be offended if I suggest that no one does masks better than those who follow Jesus?

SOME POSSIBILITIES FOR PURITY

As soon as we learn to be merciful, and before we can

move on to the practice of peace, Jesus insists we spend some time thinking about purity. He gives his sixth instruction for those who want to be his followers: "Blessed are the pure in heart."

But what kind of purity should we think about? There is a great deal said about purity in the Bible[2]—and not all of it refers to the same thing. Although some form of cleanliness is usually in mind, purity describes everything from moral rectitude and ritualistic correctness to the healing of lepers and the condition of the linen used to wrap the body of Jesus.[3] So when we stumble onto this statement—"Blessed are the *pure* in heart"—we tend to dump the whole load into this one verse. Anything we've ever heard about purity gets piled into this single statement about the pure in heart. No wonder we're confused about what Jesus means here.

One

kind of purity the Bible talks about is *ceremonial* purity. Foods are pure (clean) or impure (unclean), as are certain animals and places and body parts. When the Jews washed their hands before eating, made particular sacrifices, or changed their clothes, they were purifying themselves from ceremonial contamination. The majority of times the word pure is used in the Old Testament, it carries this connotation.

But since it's the pure *in heart* Jesus singles out in this Beatitude (and since Jesus never had much use for any kind of purity that was primarily external), it seems unlikely that ceremonial purity is what Jesus is blessing here.

The Bible also speaks frequently of *moral* purity. This purity has to do with freedom from sin and the taint of immorality. "Create in me a pure heart," wrote David after his sin with Bathsheba.[4] "Keep yourself pure," Paul said to Timothy.[5] As disciples, we're told to "purify ourselves from everything that contaminates body and spirit, perfecting holiness out of reverence for God."[6] Each of these references connects purity with righteousness, making us wonder if Jesus, in the sixth Beatitude, is blessing disciples who live holy lives.

But that's a problem—for at least two reasons.

Hasn't Jesus already said that a disciple ought to hunger and thirst for righteousness? If Jesus is talking about righteousness when he says, "Blessed are the pure in heart," he's repeating something he's already covered. Squeezing the essence of discipleship into eight core ideas is challenging enough—there's simply no room for redundancy where the Beatitudes are concerned. Jesus must mean something different when he talks about the pure in heart.

There's another reason for rethinking what purity means in this Beatitude—and it has to do with the structure we've discovered in these statements. Remember that the first four Beatitudes take us *up* to the presence of God while the second four lead us back *down* to the people we live among every day. Mercy, purity of heart, peacemaking, and suffering persecution describe how disciples interact with other people. Whatever Jesus means here by purity, he's talking about something we demonstrate to the people around us.

THE "WYSIWYG" BRAND OF PURITY

The characteristic modern malady is not plain and unvarnished materialism but sham spirituality.
—IRVING BABBITT

There's a third meaning for purity found in the Bible—not as common or obvious as ceremonial and moral cleanliness, but more helpful as we try to understand the sixth Beatitude. It has to do with *purity of motive* and builds on the notion of integrity.

Occasionally purity is used in the Bible to mean undivided, without mixture or pretense, authentic, and honest. Wine is pure if there is nothing added to dilute or water down its essence. A leper is pure when he can show himself to a priest and demonstrate that he is hiding no disease. Pure gold is unalloyed; it has integrity.

In the same way, people are said to be pure in the Bible when their actions are genuine and not prompted by false motives. Pure people behave sincerely and don't pretend to be what they're not.

In Psalms, for example, worshippers were pure when they came to the temple without ulterior motives or competing commitments.

Who may ascend the hill of the
    LORD?
Who may stand in his holy
    place?
He who has clean hands and a
    pure heart,
who does not lift up his soul to
    an idol
or swear by what is false.[7]

WYSIWYG
"What you see is what you get." A computer term for the correlation between what you see on screen and what you get on a printed page. The latest applications are able to display layout, graphics, and typefaces with accuracy. However, resolution and color matching remain problematic.
— www.pcwebopedia.com

Here it's not morality that concerns David, but *genuineness*. He insists that purity of heart prohibits secret allegiances with idols and what is false. There can be no hidden agendas for the pure. They're not permitted to cross their fingers at the temple, making private pledges that invalidate their public professions.[8]

James and Paul and the Gospel writers also use purity in this sense.[9] Taken together, these writers employ the word "pure" to describe people of integrity, people who have put away falsehood and pretense, people who want to be rid of ulterior motives and divided interests. The pure in heart are those who have dedicated themselves to living lives of sincerity.

J. B. Phillips took this understanding of the word "pure" and applied it to the sixth Beatitude in his paraphrase of the New Testament:

SINCERE

An adjective, from the Latin *sincerus*—clean, pure, sincere.
1. free from deceit, hypocrisy, or falseness; earnest
2. genuine; unfeigned
3. pure; unmixed; unadulterated
4. sound; unimpaired

—The Random House College Dictionary

Happy are the utterly sincere, for they will see God.[10]

In his wonderful commentary on the Beatitudes, William Barclay approached purity of heart from a similar perspective:

Blessed is the man whose thoughts and motives are absolutely unmixed, and, therefore, absolutely pure.[11]

So as we read this Beatitude, we should hear Jesus commenting not on our morality and certainly not on our rituals, but on our integrity. Are we on the inside what we appear to be on the outside? Are our motives pure? Do we live honest lives?

Which brings us back to the painful subject of masks.

WHY IS THE CHURCH ALWAYS THE LAST TO KNOW?

A man may cry
Church! Church!
At ev'ry word,
With no more

piety than other people—
A crow's not reckoned a
religious bird
Because it keeps a-cawing
from a steeple.

—Thomas Hood

Sincerity is commendable. It's great to be genuine. Honesty really is the best policy. Only, to tell the truth, we'd rather lie. We love our masks too much to throw them away in favor of purity.

Given half a chance, we'll lie to God. "It wasn't me, Lord." "I didn't know any better." "I'll never do that again." We forget that he sees through us, no matter how elaborate our masks become. We forget his X-ray vision that burns through our façades to the depths of our hidden hearts. There's enough arrogance in each of us to think we can fool God at least some of the time.

We'll even lie to ourselves. "I'm in control of this vice." "I'm doing this for her own good, not

---

TELL NO LIES

Sanjida O'Connell spent five months investigating the art of lying for a book called *Mindreading.* Her results? Women make more believable liars than men. And good-looking people are more likely to be believed than ... well ... the rest of us. The moral to this research? Never believe a beautiful woman.

—The Age

because I'm jealous of her." "Just this one time, and then never again." We don't mind a little self-deception now and then. We figure we can get away with fooling ourselves on occasion.

We especially love to lie to the people around us. And we lie best by means of the masks we wear. Fooling other people is what masks are all about. It's so easy to slip on that second face that keeps others from seeing the heart beneath. It's so preferable to put our best foot forward, never show weakness, and keep up the pretense of our own perfection. Masks permit us to go out in public without feeling ashamed. Who needs purity when it's so easy to play the hypocrite?

Our favorite masks are intimately connected to our use of the word "fine." Christians are partial to fine. We use that word with great frequency—and to great effect. We've

HYPOCRITE

This Greek word once referred to stage actors or those who delivered speeches. Long before New Testament times, however, the term hypocrite was extended to anyone who played a part or pretended. The word quickly developed connotations of deceit and dishonesty. In contemporary English, hypocrite denotes an insincere person, especially someone who pretends to be pious or virtuous when really not.

—Dictionary of Jesus and the Gospels

learned to deflect every inquiry into the darker corners of our lives with a reflexive "Fine."

We use it when asked about our children, our marriages, and (especially) ourselves. It's become our favorite means of muddying the waters, keeping others from seeing the real us. Fine is a word that covers a multitude of sins.

I'm thinking of a preacher I once knew. Loved by his congregation. Respected by his peers. Powerful in the pulpit. Leading a growing, dynamic church. He was always fine. He was so together. Even his hair was perfect. Only he wasn't fine. Turns out he was systematically stealing from the church treasury to cover a growing gambling debt. The man everyone saw on Sunday mornings was very different from the man who called his bookie on Saturday afternoons and fixed the books on Sunday nights. So beautiful on the

outside, but on the inside. . . .

I once knew a man who played a prominent role among the churches of a certain city. He'd given generously to worthy causes. He'd been a great defender of the faith (or at least, the status quo). When he talked, people listened. He had all his theological ducks in a row. He was fine. Except he wasn't. Turns out he'd carried on an affair with his daughter-in-law for almost twenty years. All the while he was writing big checks and speaking with such fervent certainty, he was involved in a sin so heinous it eventually destroyed his family. He was fine on the outside, but on the inside. . . .

I'm thinking about a friend of mine. He was raised in a Christian home. Married a Christian woman. He attended church where I preached. We ate breakfast together once a week. He was always fine. Great job, lots of money, nice house, new car. Fine, fine, fine—until he

COMPULSIVE GAMBLING

Nine out of ten problem gamblers are men. Ninety-one percent of problem gamblers who paid off their gambling losses continue to gamble. Seventeen percent commit suicide. Ninety-six percent began gambling before the age of fifteen. Three out of four compulsive gamblers commit felonies because of gambling.

—www.800gambler.org

told me he had to declare bankruptcy (he'd lost money in the stock market for years). Fine, fine, fine—until he had an affair with a coworker and needed me to help him put his marriage back together. Fine, fine, fine—until, one Sunday, I preached a sermon about living out what we really believed, and he decided he didn't *really* believe any of this Jesus stuff after all. He hasn't come back to church since. Cut me off without a word. But I bet if I called him today and asked how he was doing, he would answer, "Fine."

Week after week, in churches all over the world, disciples of Jesus congregate to worship God and lie to each other. We dress so prettily. We have such polite conversations in the foyer. We come off as so successful, so secure, so sincere. We say fine every chance we get.

But I wonder how many of us are different people on the inside than we pretend to be on the outside. I wonder how much of a discrepancy there is between who we are behind the closed doors of our homes and who we are in the foyer and the pew. I wonder how many of us have our public masks so firmly in place that no one suspects the private demons raging within.

Why is the church always the last to know? Perhaps because the church doesn't make honesty easy. Too often, our fellow Christians are the last people in the world we'd confess our problems to. We've seen enough polite indifference and holier-than-thou stares to make us think twice before baring our souls. We must work harder to make our churches places where honesty is rewarded rather than punished.

But we can't blame it all on the church. There's enough pride in each of us to promote hypocrisy above purity of heart. Authenticity is less important to us than appearances. Pretense becomes an acceptable

substitute for honesty. We don't have the courage to live with integrity. We'd rather don our masks than stand naked before one another and confess, "I'm not as together, I'm not as good, I'm not as fine as I would like to be." We're only willing to be honest as long as it doesn't require us to tell the truth about ourselves.

THE ADAM SOLUTION
The man and his wife were both naked, and they felt no shame.[12]

Adam and Eve were nudists. Quite literally, what you saw was what you got with these two. But their physical nakedness was only symbolic of another, more profound nakedness. In the Garden of Eden, there were no masks, no deceptions, and no secrets. These two were pure in every sense of the word. They had no sin and so enjoyed an

ANOTHER FAMOUS NUDIST
According to legend, Lady Godiva struck a deal with her husband. She would ride naked through town if he would rescind the excessive tax levied on the citizens. Godiva asked the townspeople to protect her modesty by remaining indoors during her ride. However, a tailor named Tom watched Godiva from a window. Hence the term, "Peeping Tom."
—Microsoft Encarta

absolute moral purity before God. But neither was there anything to hide from each other—no humiliating faults, no embarrassing failures, no shame. They could afford to be naked with one another—there was nothing to cover up.

It takes sin to spark in us the desire to conceal. When Adam and Eve ate the forbidden fruit, they ceased to be innocent and began a long tradition of hiding. The first thing recorded of these two after their disobedience was an attempt to sew fig leaves together, to make "coverings for themselves." Certainly they wanted to hide from God—Adam cowered behind the nearest tree the next time God came around.

"I heard you in the garden, and I was afraid because I was naked; so I hid." [13]

But they also hid from each other. The days of being honest were over. Suddenly there were excuses and rationalizations and blaming and anger and resentments, which had to be stuffed away out of sight. Adam didn't want to show his shame to Eve. Eve couldn't afford to let Adam see too much of what she was really thinking. So they sewed fig leaves together—physically and psychologically. They hid their nakedness—body and soul.

From that day on, Adam and his children have proven themselves masters of the well-placed fig leaf. Throughout our history, we've elevated hiding to a fine art. Coverings, disguises, and masks have become the necessary accouterments of human existence. We will not be caught naked. No one will see us as we really are. There's too much in even the best of us that is best concealed.

The truth is that even disciples of Christ keep pursuing Adam's solution. We're still trying to hide the truth about ourselves behind the nearest fig leaf. We hear everyone around us saying fine, and we quickly learn to put on those little hypocrisies that make our lives appear prettier than they really are. We invent ways to deceive each other into thinking we have it all together, that we don't struggle moment by moment with specific and nasty sins. We learn to put our best face forward, even if it's not our truest face. We content ourselves with looking beautiful on the outside, no matter what kind of ugliness is bubbling within.

We have plenty of cause to fear sincerity. Stand in the church foyer and tell someone how you're *really* feeling and you'll discover a few of them: shocked looks, embarrassed grins, strained silence, dull advice, withdrawal, gossip, and judgment. But our sincerophobia goes deeper than that. Adam and Eve had no experience with poorly handled honesty. Yet they hid. So while other Christians might be our *excuse* for insincerity, the *cause* is rooted deep within ourselves.

THE NAKED DISCIPLE

If we claim to be without sin, we deceive ourselves and the truth is not in us. If we confess our sins, he is faithful and just and will forgive. . . .

—JOHN THE BELOVED

Make my breast transparent as pure crystal, that the world, jealous of me, may see the foulest thought my heart does hold.

—GEORGE VILLIERS

The purity Jesus speaks of in this Beatitude addresses not so much the *absence* of sin as the *solution* we adopt in dealing with its painful presence.

Sin, shortcomings, struggles—these are givens in a disciple's life. Though we may hunger for righteousness, we will never completely avoid the junk food that Satan substitutes.

But it's how disciples deal with sin that is at issue in the sixth Beatitude—sins from our past and (more to the point) sins in our present. Is the Christian life a constant battle to keep our masks in place and our sins secret, or is discipleship a commitment to shedding those false skins for truer faces? Are Christians eternally damned to saying fine, or would Jesus teach us a more honest word?

The antithesis of purity isn't immorality but insincerity, not the presence of sin but the denial of it. It's Adam's substitute for authentic living. It's the preference for concealment over transparency. It's the victory of masks over integrity. And every one of us is guilty of it.

But Adam's solution isn't Jesus' solution. Adam says, "Hide." Jesus says, "Be honest." Adam says, "Cover up." Jesus says, "Expose yourself." Adam says, "Play the hypocrite, wear the mask, pretend to be what you're not."

Jesus says, "Have the courage to be pure in heart."

The purity Jesus speaks of in this Beatitude invites us to take off our fig leaves and go naked once again. This purity involves the willingness to turn ourselves inside out, to let people see not the façade, but the heart. It requires the courage to be transparent, to wear our struggles on our sleeves, to be only as fine on the outside as we are in our heart of hearts. This kind of purity teaches us to show ourselves—warts and all. It thrusts us into public places without the benefit of the spiritual makeup we have used for so long to cover unsightly blemishes.

The pure live in glass houses, inviting and welcoming the inspection of others. The pure have nothing to hide—or rather, will hide nothing. The pure have dedicated themselves to live sincerely before others. The pure have the courage to go naked before the world, testifying to God's goodness by giving glimpses in their own lives of his transforming power and forgiving grace. With the pure, what you see is what you get—the unvarnished person, the unedited version, the genuine article.

FOR THEY SHALL SEE GOD

Hateful to me even as the gates of Hades is he that hideth one thing in his heart and uttereth another.
—HOMER, *ILIAD*

The promise attached to the sixth Beatitude involves epiphany. The pure will see God. I suggest that is Jesus' way of saying, "It takes one to know one."

Our God is a revealing God. His desire is to make himself known. He shows himself in his words, in his actions, and in his Son. There's nothing about our Father that he'd hide from us. He has no dark secrets to conceal. There are no ulterior motives in his love for us. There are many things we don't know about God, but that's due to our incapacity rather than his lack of candor.

Our ability to see what God reveals about himself is directly linked to the kind of eyes we're looking through. The thief imagines that everyone is stealing from him. The adulterer is always suspicious of his wife. The murderer sees an assassin in every face. What does the mask-wearer, the hidden man, the hypocrite see when he looks at God?

Many Christians are convinced there's less to God than meets the eye. Though they would never admit it, their theology owes more to *The Wizard of Oz* than to the Bible. Behind God's booming voice and powerful deeds is a little man pulling levers. They suspect this is true of God because they know it's true of themselves.

They hear God say, "You're forgiven. Your sins have been washed away. The price has been paid," but they're suspicious of grace. They keep looking this gift-God in the mouth. They're certain the

other shoe is about to drop. God cannot be as gracious as he appears. There must be another God behind that merciful mask.

Or they hear God say, "I will transform you into my image. I will create Christ within you," but they find that hard to believe. So they settle for a form of godliness while "denying its power."[14] They substitute rules and regulations that "lack any value in restraining sensual indulgence" for the transformative power of dying and being raised with Christ.[15] God may say one thing, but he means another.

People who wear masks spend their lives trying to rip the mask off God. They never trust God completely because they fully expect they've not been told the whole story. Seeing is never really believing for those who are not pure themselves. They, of all people, know how easy it is to cover ugly realities with an illusion. That's why only the pure in

THE WIZARD OF OZ

Frank Morgan portrayed the diminutive Professor Marvel (the Wizard) in the classic 1939 movie starring Judy Garland. When "unveiled," the fearsome Wizard turned out to be a rather embarrassed and apologetic old man.

heart see God—really see him. It takes a pure person to believe in a pure God. Only those who have learned to live without subterfuge can trust what God reveals about himself. Only those who have renounced masks to wear their true faces are able to take God at face value.

And so we trace this simple circle. Who are the pure in heart? They're people who have the courage to be honest about themselves with others. The practice of honesty with others grants them the courage to be more honest with themselves. Honesty with self is required to be honest with God. And only those who are honest with God can believe that God is being honest with them. "Blessed are the pure in heart, for they will see God."

TOP TEN . . .

TOP TEN WAYS TO PRACTICE PRETENSE IN PLACE OF PURITY

10. Learn to fake sincerity.

9. Carry a Bible at all times—a pocket edition that can be easily hidden.

8. Determine never to go to R-rated movies (at least not with other Christians).

7. When hearing someone confess a sin, always respond with, "I don't struggle with that personally, but. . . ."

6. Convince yourself that Abraham Lincoln was wrong—you really *can* fool all of the people all of the time.

5. When you can't be good, have a good alibi.

4. Dress nicely. An expensive outfit covers a multitude of sins.

3. When in doubt, deny. When denying, sound earnest (see #10 above).

2. Never do anything you'd be ashamed to be caught doing—unless you're absolutely certain no one is watching.

And the **#1** way to practice pretense rather than purity:

Install a quick-release latch on your "What Would Jesus Do?" bracelet.

THE STORY OF . . .

Monseigneur Bienvenu

THE PURE PRIEST

Perhaps you've seen the play or heard the soundtrack. You might even have read the book (in the *Cliff's Notes* version if not the entire work). Victor Hugo's *Les Misérables* has enjoyed something of a comeback recently when an adaptation of the book hit Broadway.

The book itself, while brilliant, is long. The edition I possess runs more than twelve hundred pages—and it is an abridgement of the original. Hugo was merciless to his readers. He left out nothing. "Les Mis" is full of digressions and asides and irrelevant historical trivia.

And I'm thankful for it. For without Hugo's lack of discipline, we never would have met Monseigneur Bienvenu, bishop of Digne. His only role in the story is to offer an act of kindness to an ex-convict (Jean Valjean) and to plant the seed for a better way of living. But to set up that single act, Hugo requires almost one hundred pages, exploring in detail the character and career of the good bishop.

Along the way, Hugo paints a word picture of a truly pure man. As Hugo portrays him, this bishop is one of the most attractive characters in all of literature.

Bienvenu was old, about seventy-five, when the events of the novel begin. He served the people of Digne as their bishop, preaching and ministering to this quiet diocese in southeastern France. He spent only what was required to keep himself alive and attend to his duties—the rest of his income was distributed to the poor and various good works. He was humble in his dealings with others and gentle with their failings. He was capable of great acts of kindness, showing mercy where others had turned their backs and reaching out to those who had nowhere else to turn. He was incorruptible and totally without worldly ambition.

In a time and culture where corruption among priests was commonplace, Bienvenu was a shining exception.

But it's the man's *purity* that is most striking to me. In describing Bienvenu, Hugo portrayed someone who had no illusions about himself, no pretense or hypocrisy, no need to cover up. Bienvenu was a naked man. He readily confessed his flaws. He told the truth about himself. Struggling sinners found in this priest not a critic, but a fellow struggler. Mercy flowed out of him because he knew himself to be so much in need of mercy. He was honest—not just about others but, most particularly, about himself.

Being, as he said with a smile, himself a former sinner, he lacked all sanctimoniousness, and without self-righteous flourishes preached in forthright terms.

His position entitled him to certain honors and deference. But he would have none of it. He refused to wrap himself in the mantle of his office. Instead, he went out to greet the world in the most genuine and unpretentious way.

Bienvenu was a man whose motives were pure, a man who wouldn't hide, a sincere and authentic man. As a result, his people loved him deeply. They loved him for his humble, unassuming manner. They loved that he was a good man who did not consider himself better than others. They loved that their bishop was willing to share not only his wisdom and compassion, but also his struggles.

Such people are rare in our world. In fact, they're so rare that it was easier for me to draw from fiction than from real life to illustrate what a pure person looks like. But they're out there. Some of them are preachers and priests. Some are parents. Some are business people and doctors. Some are custodians. The pure can be found among the rich and the poor, the old and the young, the educated and the illiterate. What they have in common isn't race or income or position. It's the willingness to be honest about themselves. It's the courage to let people see into them. It's the integrity to allow their own lives to be their greatest testimony to the goodness of God.

You might want to dust off your copy of *Les Misérables* and reread the first hundred pages. See if you don't agree with me about Monseigneur Bienvenu. And then see if you can be more like him.

THINKING IT THROUGH

MONDAY

There's something about the person of Jesus that makes honesty about ourselves both necessary and easy. People didn't hide much from Jesus. They were quick to speak the truth about themselves in his presence. Look at the following examples and think about these questions. What was it in Jesus that prompted these confessions? Why did people "come clean" when they spent time around him? How did Jesus respond to such expressions?

- Luke 5:8—Peter's confession
- Luke 7:1-7—A centurion who isn't worthy
- Luke 7:36-38—A woman weeps her confession
- Luke 19:1-10—Zacchaeus repents
- Luke 23:39-43—A thief confesses

TUESDAY

The early church was a place where people could afford to be honest about themselves. The following passages show the reality of this honesty in New Testament communities of faith. Read these verses and then ask yourself, "Are the same things happening in my church today?"

- Acts 19:17-20—Ephesian Christians confess
- Ephesians 4:25; James 5:16— Encouragement to confess to fellow Christians
- Acts 26:9-11; 1 Corinthians 15:9-10; 2 Corinthians 12:7-10; Galatians 1:13; 1 Timothy 1:13-16—Paul is transparent about his past
- 2 Corinthians 1:12; 4:2; 1 Thessalonians 2:3-6,8; Philippians 1:7-8—Examples of Paul's "plainness" with his converts
- 1 John 1:8-10—Denial versus confession
- 1 Corinthians 5:1-2— Too much openness?

WEDNESDAY

This kind of honesty (whether about failings or feelings) requires an environment where such expressions are encouraged. Paul tried to build this kind of environment in the churches he wrote to. As you look at the following passages, think about how these recommended attitudes and behaviors would make telling the truth easier. You might want to write down particular recommendations for further study and prayer.

- Romans 12:15-18; 15:1-2
- Galatians 6:1-5
- Ephesians 4:1-3,29,32
- Philippians 2:3-4
- Colossians 3:12-15
- 1 Thessalonians 5:14-15

THURSDAY

There are plenty of biblical examples of people who were dishonest about themselves, who couldn't tell the truth where their own hearts were concerned. Read the following passages. What were these people hiding? Why were they hiding it? What was the result?

- Matthew 23:25-28 — The Pharisees
- Acts 5:1-11 — Ananias and Sapphira
- Romans 16:17-18 — Those who cause division
- 1 Corinthians 3:18-20 — Those who think they're wise
- 2 Timothy 4:2-4 — Those with itching ears

FRIDAY

Sincerity is frequently mentioned in the New Testament. Read the following references and meditate on the importance of this attribute. You might also note how often sincerity is coupled with purity in these readings. Pray through these verses — asking God to purify your heart and grant you an honest, earnest, and genuine spirit.

- Romans 12:9-10
- 1 Corinthians 5:8;11:3
- Ephesians 6:5
- 1 Timothy 1:5; 3:8
- Hebrews 10:22
- James 3:17
- 1 Peter 1:22

What was the most significant lesson you learned in your study this week?

TALKING IT OVER

TEXT: MATTHEW 3:1-6; JOHN: 1:6-9,19-27; 3:22-30

WARM-UP:

Have you ever pretended to be something you're not?

Most of us are guilty from time to time of putting on false fronts, appearing to be better or smarter or stronger than we really are. We often exaggerate a little in our own favor.

Can you tell of a time when you weren't yourself? Maybe you were interviewing for a job or dating someone you really wanted to impress. Maybe there are times at church or in your family life you're tempted to dispense with honesty in favor of a mask. When do you find yourself most vulnerable to do this?

Let's discuss purity and the importance of telling the truth about ourselves. In preparation, have one of the group members read about John the Baptist from Matthew 3:1-6; John 1:6-9,19-27; 3:22-30.

DISCUSSION:

First, develop a profile of John:

1. What was John's blood relationship with Jesus?
2. What was John's mission? How did he receive this mission?
3. How many people went to hear John's preaching? What kind of people did John preach to? Would you call John successful?
4. Did John ever have an opportunity to pretend to be something he was not?
5. What (or who) could he have pretended to be?
6. Did the crowds seem eager to make John something more than he knew himself to be (see Luke 3:15)?
7. John would not have been the first man to believe everything the crowds were saying about him. Do you think he was tempted? What kept him grounded in who he was and what he came to do?

John is perhaps the most sincere and honest person we meet in Scripture besides Jesus.

Look at the many ways in which he demonstrated his purity to anyone who would listen.

1. How many people, pretending to be better than they really are, would live in the desert, wear a loin cloth, and feed on locusts and wild honey?
2. When people tried to make John the Messiah, or the Prophet, or Elijah, what was his consistent response?
3. When Jesus came on the scene, how did John tell the truth about him? Do you see John deflecting attention away from himself and onto Jesus? How?

One of the finest moments in John's life comes when he says of Jesus, "He must become greater; I must become less." John appears to be utterly lacking in pretense. Would you agree?

APPLICATION:

1. What if you were John the Baptist and people were flocking to hear you preach, saying flattering things about you, and

wanting to follow you. How would you have handled that?

2. Do you tend to downplay or to exaggerate yourself? Do you deflect attention from yourself or gather as much attention as you can? Be honest. Maybe someone in the group who knows you well should answer this question for you.

3. In this self-assertive, look-out-for-yourself world, it's not easy to cultivate honesty about ourselves even when it hurts. To bluntly tell others, "I'm not who you think I am," is hard. Would you agree?

4. John had a real sense of who he was and who he was not. And he always told the truth about both matters. How can you and I develop a better sense of ourselves so that we can be honest and pure?

5. What is your favorite device for hiding the truth about yourself? Perhaps it's bragging or white lies or a barrier you allow no one to penetrate. What can you do this week to be more honest with others?

COOL DOWN:

John chose to be honest about himself. We can too. But doing so requires us to value honesty more than the approval and admiration of others. Commit to the members of the group that you'll try to tell the truth about yourself this week.

Perhaps the most practical way of doing this is to keep in mind John's statement, "He must become greater; I must become less." Spending your time ensuring that Jesus is honored rather than yourself is a good first step toward an open life. End this discussion by praying for God to help you deflect more attention away from yourself and toward him.

LIVING IT OUT

It's funny how virtues can so easily become vices.

It happens all too often with the desire to be pure in heart. Confession results in alienation rather than understanding. Sharing struggles causes strain rather than easing tensions. You talk about yourself honestly and somebody beats you over the head and shoulders with what you say.

If we're to practice purity of heart, a bit of wisdom has to be mixed with our honesty. Ambushing people in the church foyer with the sordid details of your struggles with lust may be sincere, but it's also stupid. You can only give people as much honesty as they can stand. Ultimately, purity of heart isn't about personal catharsis or dumping your failures on unsuspecting listeners.

Purity of heart is honesty put to use for building others up.

You have to be a good listener to be pure in heart. You have to gauge what others need, what they can stand, and what would encourage them before purity of heart becomes a useful skill. Sincerity

doesn't happen in a vacuum. It requires your honest heart and someone else's receptive ear.

Here's one simple way you can practice purity wisely. Each of us has accumulated a lifetime of stories. They come from relationships, experiences, mistakes, and successes. Some are funny. Some are sad. Some are painful and even tragic. One way of practicing purity is through telling these stories.

But the point of purity isn't to go around boring people by constantly telling stories about yourself. The point is to tell stories *strategically*, to share things from your own life that will bless those who hear.

So the next time you're in conversation with a fellow Christian and you feel an irresistible urge to commit purity, think about the following steps.

Listen—Focus on the other person (always a good thing for Christians to practice). Hear what he or she is saying. Try to hear beyond the words to the need.

Remember—Think of stories from your own life that sound

similar to what you're hearing. Sort through them until you come to the one story that is most appropriate to what you're hearing.

Share—This is where the purity comes out. Tell a story from your life. It might be a story of failure. It might be embarrassing to you. It might involve confession. Who cares? The point is that you can be helpful to someone by risking a little transparency.

Listen—Was your story helpful? Was your friend encouraged or instructed or comforted? Did he or she respond with even greater honesty and sincerity? By asking such questions, you can determine whether your efforts at purity were a burden or a blessing.

This week, take a very small piece of paper (maybe the smallest Post-It note) and write these four words on it: Listen, Remember, Share, Listen. Now tape it around your watch band so you'll see it frequently. As you go through your week—especially as you find yourself in conversations with others—let this list guide you as you try to interact in a pure, straightforward, and honest way.

The following prayer might help you become a person who is pure in heart.

Father,
So much of my life has been spent hiding—from myself, from others, and, especially, from you. I'm weary of the masks, dear Lord. I'm tired of the pretense.

Create a pure heart within me, O God. Give me the courage to be done with falsehood and hypocrisy. Help me to walk among your people in sincerity. Teach me to use my life, with all its scars, to give others hope and comfort. Help me to share myself in such a way that others are blessed and you are glorified.

Your greatest gifts have been the healing of my deepest wounds. You are at your best when I am at my worst. Your grace covers a multitude of my sins. I want to speak of such matters so that, in confessing my brokenness, I can bear testimony to your mercies. Amen.

IN A WORD

Purity of heart declares,

"I will speak the truth to you."

It's the willingness to share ourselves with others, to be open and sincere, to live transparent lives.

It's honesty put to use for the benefit of others and the glory of God.

Give PEACE a CHANCE

Yes we love peace but we are not willing to take wounds for it as we are for war.

—JOHN ANDREW HOLMES

During the Middle East War of 1948, when the Jews were fighting to establish the modern state of Israel and their Arab neighbors were fighting to prevent it, Warren Austin—then U.S. ambassador to the United Nations—stood before the Assembly to urge Arabs and Jews to resolve their disagreements "like good Christians."[1]

Not only did he show amazing insensitivity to his audience, he also displayed a towering ignorance of history and the manner in which "good Christians" have frequently resolved their differences. The long history of Christianity has not been a peaceful one. We have shown ourselves willing to sacrifice peace for almost any cause. We'll fight at the drop of a dogma. Challenge our comfort zones and we'll beat the war drums. Question our prac-

tices and we'll call out the cavalry. It doesn't take much for us to send peace packing. Throughout the centuries and by some strange alchemy, peace has been transformed from one of the central concerns of the Christian religion to an expendable luxury Christians can afford to toss overboard whenever faith springs a leak.

> ### JEWISH-ARAB WARS
> Although fighting has been almost constant since Israel declared its existence in 1947, there have been three major wars between Israel and its Arab neighbors in the past fifty years: the War of Independence (1948), the Six Day War (1967), and the Yom Kippur War (1973).
>
> *— War, Peace, and Security Guide*

"Blessed are the peacemakers, for they will be called sons of God."

Yet we feel guilty—about both our conflicted history and our conflicted attitudes toward peace. At some level we're well aware that peace is more important to the heart of God than we have made it in our homes and churches. It's hard to see any trace of God in the Crusades or the Inquisition, or in turf wars over TV ministries and pastoral power bases. We're sad that—in the name of religion—violent things still are being said and done, from car bombings in Jerusalem to character assassinations in local churches. No matter how sacred the cause, we suspect God leaves in disgust just before the fists start to fly.

It's probably fair to say that all of us have an uneasy relationship with peace. We're ashamed of our tendency to war, yet proud of the fact that there are things we believe deeply enough to fight for. We know we ought to value peace more highly, but sense that a peace purchased at any price is too expensive. We long to live more peaceably with others, but realize that not everyone desires to live in peace with us. We're all for peace in principle; it's peace in practice that gives us fits.

WAR AND PEACE IN THE LIFE OF JESUS

I believe it to be a grave mistake to present Christianity as something charming and popular with no offence in it. . . . Whatever [Christ's] peace was, it was not the peace of an amiable indifference.

—Dorothy Leigh Sayers

Our own ambivalence about Christian peace is rooted in a corresponding ambiguity in the life of

Christ. Jesus came preaching, "Peace, peace." But you don't have to search very hard in the Gospels to know there was no peace (or, at least, not much of it) in his own ministry.

Isaiah named the Messiah the "Prince of Peace" six hundred years before Jesus was born. When he comes, said the prophet, the wolf will lie down with the lamb,[2] and "of the increase of his peace" there will be no end.[3] But Isaiah's portrait of the peaceable kingdom is sandwiched by other, less peaceable images. The very first prophecy in the Bible related to the Messiah uses violent rather than pastoral imagery: "He will crush [the serpent's] head."[4] And the very last prophecy in the Bible in which Jesus makes an appearance is even more graphically warlike:

I saw heaven standing open and there before me was a white horse, whose rider is called Faithful and True. With justice he judges and makes war. His eyes are like blazing

fire.... He is dressed in a robe dipped in blood, and his name is the Word of God. The armies of heaven were following him, riding on white horses and dressed in fine linen, white and clean. Out of his mouth comes a sharp sword with which to strike down the nations. "He will rule them with an iron scepter." He treads the winepress of the fury of the wrath of God Almighty.[5]

At the birth of Jesus, the heavenly host proclaimed, "Peace on earth!"[6] But forty days later, an old man took the child into his arms and predicted:

This child is destined to cause the falling and rising of many in Israel, and to be a sign that will be spoken against, so that the thoughts of many hearts will be revealed.[7]

Throughout his ministry, Jesus preached "Peace!"[8] He promised to give peace.[9] He encouraged his disciples to "be at peace with each other."[10] He commanded his disciples to forgive each other and reconcile with those who felt alienated. He insisted that they love their enemies and bless those who cursed them, turn the other cheek and not resist an evil person.

Yet this Prince of Peace would tell his disciples:

"Do not suppose that I have come to bring peace to the earth. I did not come to bring peace, but a sword."[11]

He made other statements that, for someone who claimed to love peace, seem polarizing ("He who is not with me is against me"[12]) and confrontive ("No one who puts his hand to the plow and looks back is fit for service in the kingdom of God"[13]).

But it's especially in his clashes with the Pharisees that we're made to wonder just what kind of peace Jesus came to champion. The interactions between Jesus and the Pharisees, though they began with the polite parry and thrust of theological discussion, quickly degenerated into a battle to the death. His verbal joustings with this group were frequent and acerbic. He expected no quarter in arguments with them—and gave little in return.

"Woe to you, teachers of the law and Pharisees, you hypocrites! You shut the kingdom of heaven in men's faces. You yourselves do not enter, nor will you let those enter who are trying to. . . . You travel over land and sea to win a single convert, and when he becomes one, you make him twice as much a son of hell as you are. . . . Woe to you, blind guides! . . . You blind fools! . . . You strain out a gnat but swallow a camel. . . . You are like whitewashed tombs, which look beautiful on the outside but on the inside are full of dead men's bones and everything unclean. . . . You snakes! You brood of vipers! How will you escape being condemned to hell?"[14]

NO QUARTER

According to an ancient agreement between the Dutch and the Spaniards, captured soldiers could be ransomed by paying a fee equal to one quarter of their annual pay. Thus, "to grant quarter" meant to spare the life of an enemy in your power. "No quarter," on the other hand, meant that no mercy would be shown—the captured soldier could be killed or sold into slavery.

—The Dictionary of Phrase and Fable

The Pharisees killed Jesus out of self-protection. They felt threatened, condemned, and belittled by him. It wasn't the peaceable Jesus they nailed to the cross, but the argumentative one. Jesus may have preached peace, but he did so using the rhetoric of revolution.

WHO IS THE PEACEMAKER?

I am a man of peace. I believe in peace. But I do not want peace at any price.
—MAHATMA GANDHI

So what does Jesus mean when he says, "Blessed are the peacemakers"? Just who are these people? What kind of person is Jesus describing? The one thing we must avoid with this Beatitude is resorting to simplistic platitudes that gloss over the real complexities of Christian peace.

Some people will tell you that Jesus wants disciples who are the kind of easygoing, good-natured folks who get along with everyone. But what, then, do we do with Jesus himself? I wouldn't exactly call Jesus easygoing. And there were more than a few people he didn't get along with very well.

Is Jesus suggesting that disciples never get upset or angry? Some Christians insist that followers of Jesus must not show any sign of temper, that wrath has no place in the life of a peacemaker. Again, what about Jesus? He could and did get angry. He gave angry glances[15] and spoke angry words and once made a whip to drive people bodily from the temple![16]

Are peacemakers people who will have peace at any cost, who will swallow any indignity, who will go to any length to avoid conflict? Listening to some of us talk, you'd think that Jesus wants only disciples who would sooner surrender than fight. But that certainly doesn't describe what we see in our Lord. There were some things more important to Jesus than

THE PEACEMAKER

Produced from 1873-1940—and used by such Western legends as Wyatt Earp and Doc Holliday—the .45 caliber Colt Peacemaker was the gun that won the Old West. The B-36—the largest bomber ever put into service by the U.S. Air Force—was also named the Peacemaker. In the mid-1980s, a ballistic missile capable of delivering ten independently targeted nuclear warheads was named the PeaceKeeper. Why are weapons of war designated with names beginning with the word "peace"?

peace and calm.

It's within the context of Christ's life that we must hear his words, "Blessed are the peacemakers." Whatever peacemaking means, it should be defined by our Lord's life and behavior—not twisted to mean something that makes nonsense of the peace he practiced. Jesus embodies the essence of a peacemaker—he doesn't ask us to practice what he can only preach. If there seems to be some disparity between the Prince of Peace and his practice of peace, the disparity exists in our understanding of peace rather than in his attempts to make it.

This much is clear: The peace Jesus tells us to make is not the flaccid pacifism too often proclaimed from pulpits and in religious writings. Nor is it just a pious principle that can be jettisoned whenever it becomes inconvenient. Jesus is calling us to take peace seriously, but to think carefully about when and where we commit peace.

PEACEMAKING AS A PRIVATE VIRTUE

Peace is such a precious jewel that I would give anything for it but truth.

—MATTHEW HENRY

In chapter six we said, "The true measure of a disciple is not whether you can make it into the presence of God, but whether you can take God's presence back down to the marketplace and the home and the church." In these final four Beatitudes, we're walking back down the mountain of God to the plane of daily life—away from a purely vertical religion (one practiced exclusively between ourselves and God) and toward a religion that makes a horizontal difference (affecting the way we relate to the people around us).

With that in mind, we should expect peacemaking to have a distinctly interpersonal bent. It's not peace within ourselves or even peace with God that concerns Jesus here, but peace with the people around us. Those who demonstrate compassion (mercy) and integrity (purity) in their relationships with other people are now called upon to make and keep the peace in those relationships.

But which relationships? Jesus had a relationship with the Pharisees, but it wasn't peaceful. He had a relationship with the crowds, but more were offended by Jesus than persuaded to become followers. Jesus could be a peacemaker and still not get along with everybody he knew.

As Jesus leads us back down the mountain, I suggest that he takes us first through crowded places and then to the more intimate relationships of our private lives. Each evening after work, you drive through the city and neighborhood before

you can get home. These final Beatitudes seem to work in a similar way. They move us from the realm of strangers and passing acquaintances to the realm of friends and family and fellowship.

We, of course, want to move in the opposite direction. Take the fifth and sixth Beatitudes (mercy and purity of heart), for example. Here Jesus describes virtues that we'd love to limit to our private lives. We want to reserve compassion and honesty for a handful of best-loved people. But Jesus drags those virtues out into the public arena. He asks us to show compassion and integrity to everyone—even people we don't know, even our enemies. Though these two virtues are certainly appropriate at home, the point Jesus makes is that they don't end there. They must be demonstrated when disciples are on the road and among strangers.

Now, as we consider the last two Beatitudes, we come to virtues we're tempted to make public. Peacemaking

THE COMMUTER CALCULATOR

Would you like to know how much your daily commute costs (in both dollars and pollutants)? Check out this website: www.magic.ca/iclei/games/comcalc.html

becomes a puppy's eagerness to make friends with anyone and persecution is something inflicted by strangers and faceless enemies of the faith. As we'll see, though, Jesus is talking about something closer to home. These Beatitudes describe virtues that disciples display best in the intimate places of our lives.

That's certainly true of peacemaking. Jesus isn't asking us to get along with everyone. But he is telling us that we must protect and preserve some relationships. Though we will always have enemies,[17] there are certain kinds of relationships in which Christ's followers must not only want peace, but make it.

WHAT KIND OF PEACEMAKER WAS JESUS?

All men desire peace, but few desire the things that make for peace.

—THOMAS À KEMPIS

The Jesus we meet in the Gospels was open to living at peace with most people—though he'd fight if forced to it. But there were certain people Jesus was *determined* to live at peace with, people he wouldn't give up on or go to war with. In his relationship with the disciples, we see Jesus move beyond an openness to peace to a commitment to peacemaking.

Jesus is a peacemaker because of the way he interacts with the Twelve.

His patience with and commitment to the apostles is a source of constant (and comforting) amazement. These were the people Jesus had an intimate relationship with. They were his friends, his fellowship, his family. They and he were joined to each other. For better or worse, in life or in death, God had glued them together with a bond Jesus wouldn't break.

Take Simon Peter, for example. Peter was not an easy man to live with. Headstrong, loud-mouthed, impetuous, and crude, Peter's bumblings are strewn throughout the Gospel accounts. When we first meet Peter in the gospel of Luke, he warns Jesus to stay away from him—by his own admission, he's "a sinful man."[18] He sinks when attempting to walk on water.[19] He fails to understand when Jesus teaches in parables.[20] He struggles with the concept of forgiveness.[21]

Any one of these failings might have disqualified Peter as a member of the inner circle—had you or I been in charge. But when you add to them the disastrous string of blunders committed by Peter during the final days of Jesus' life, you expect to hear even Jesus lose patience.

"Peter! I told you about the cross and you rebuked me. I tried to wash your feet and you refused me. I predicted your desertion

SUPERGLUE
Cyanoacrylates were discovered by accident during World War II when, attempting to develop a clear plastic for gunsights, Dr. Harry Coover ran onto a material that stuck to everything it contacted. "It was a severe pain." It wasn't until 1951, however, when Coover worked with Dr. Fred Joyner (the perfect name!) that the idea of using the substance as a glue developed.

—www.telusplanet.net/public/
jwberger/scient~1.html

and you rebuffed me. I said you'd deny me and you ridiculed the very notion. Well, Peter, I've had it with you. You've disappointed me once too often. I'll have to find someone else to be my rock. Pack your bags. You're out of here!"

That's probably what I would have said. And that's what we often say to people less flawed than Peter. But not Jesus. Jesus saw Peter through the lens of commitment, and it moved him to make peace with Peter where we might have expected relational war.

Peter says, "Go away from me, Lord!" Jesus says, "Don't be afraid; from now on you'll catch men."[22] Peter sinks, but Jesus reaches out his hand to save him.[23] Peter doesn't get the parable (even Jesus says he's dull), but then Jesus takes the time to explain so Peter will understand.[24] Peter rebukes Jesus for talking about a cross,[25] but "six days later" Jesus asks Peter to go with him to the Mount of Transfigura-

tion.[26] Peter sleeps when he should be praying, fights when he should submit, runs when he ought to stay, and denies when he needs to confess.[27] But the risen Jesus reinstates the fallen Peter and invites him to "Feed my sheep."[28]

Jesus never gives up on Peter. He could have. Some would say he should have. But it was precisely because he chose to reconcile with Peter—to value the relationship enough to deal with the problems—that Jesus could claim to be a peacemaker and dare to challenge us to be the same.

You see this passion for peace come out with the rest of the disciples as well. When James and John maneuver for the chief seats and want to call down fire from heaven on the Samaritans,[29] when Thomas doubts,[30] when Philip can't imagine where they might get bread to feed the multitudes or fails to recognize the Father in Jesus,[31] when all of them are terrified in the storm or bewildered by Christ's teaching or

arguing about which of them is the greatest,[32] Jesus always opts for making peace rather than drawing lines. Oh, he'll confront and rebuke. Even with those he loved, Jesus didn't shrink from conflict. But he doesn't reject his flawed disciples. He doesn't give up or turn off or let go. He may tell his disciples to leave the Pharisees alone, but he refuses to do the same for the Twelve.

This is the core of what it means to be a peacemaker. Peacemaking isn't about doing shuttle diplomacy between warring nations. It's not, primarily, a matter of refusing to take up arms against people you don't even know. It doesn't mean that you run from conflict whenever it rears its ugly head. Peacemaking takes place in the context of our most intimate relationships. It's a characteristic we demonstrate when relationships are broken, when alienation threatens, when we must choose either to reject or reconcile with someone we love.

SHUTTLE DIPLOMACY

This phrase was coined in the mid-1970s to describe Henry Kissinger's penchant for flying back and forth to negotiate agreements between sworn enemies. While leading negotiations to end the Yom Kippur War, for example, Kissinger (in the course of thirty-four days) traveled 24,230 miles on forty-one flights between Damascus, Jerusalem, and Alexandria.

— Kissinger: A Biography

PEACE—LIKE CHARITY—BEGINS AT HOME

The world will believe in peace only when the churches will demonstrate that it can exist.

—LECOMTE DU NOÜY

One of my favorite "Peanuts" cartoons has Lucy delivering that famous line: "I love the world. It's people I can't stand." As one of the more profound philosophers of our age, Lucy puts her finger on a problem we all share. It's easier to love people in the abstract than to love them up close and personal.

How true that is with peace. We want to understand peacemaking in a global context or talk about pacifism as a doctrinal position or see ourselves as the grand reconcilers of a lost world to God. But when we go home each evening, there's war in our families. We go to church on Sundays, and the conflict simmers just beneath the surface of our polite words. We speak passionately about

peace as a principle, but fail to practice peace with the people we know best.

Certainly there are implications in peacemaking for how a Christian acts in times of war or with obnoxious strangers. But the primary thrust of this Beatitude cuts closer to the bone than mere generalities. Jesus wants disciples who know how to be peacemakers with their spouses, their children, their friends, their brothers and sisters in the faith. It's particularly in our most intimate relationships that Jesus calls us to make peace. Peacemaking—like charity—begins at home.

The truth of the matter is that—even for Christians—relationships are a messy business. Like Jesus and his disciples, there are times when we don't understand the ones we care about, when disappointments and frustrations threaten to overwhelm affectionate feelings, when we're deeply hurt by the very ones we deeply love.

Conflict is relationship's Siamese twin. Though nothing would please us more than to enjoy the relationship without the conflict, the two are bound together beyond our ability to divorce them. If you want one you must accept the other. . . . It is not until we conflict that we discover whether love binds us together or merely convenience.[33]

Into every relationship, a little conflict must fall. And certain conflicts will bring relationships to a fork in the road where choices must be made. Will we elect to forgive or resent, apologize or rationalize, reconcile or reject? Will we say, "Enough is enough," or find a way to make peace?

What distinguishes followers of Christ from the world are not perfect relationships or the absence of conflicts, but the way disciples treat each other when relationships become strained. Christians—serious Christians—take peace seriously. They respond to the breakdown of relationship with a reflexive urge to reconcile.

FAMILIARITY BREEDS CONTEMPT?

Between 1980 and 1994, the number of whites killed by acquaintances increased 44 percent, while the number of blacks killed by acquaintances jumped 115 percent. Husbands and boyfriends are responsible for 26 percent of female homicides.

—U.S. Department of Justice

That urge to reconcile is the essence of peacemaking. In contrast to the disposable relationships we see in the world around us, Christian relationships have a permanence that only regular maintenance and a willingness to make repairs can bestow. Rather than exchanging broken relationships for shiny new ones, disciples lovingly restore relationships they value too much to throw away. When once-healthy marriages or friendships or spiritual companionships begin to sicken and wither, disciples respond by nursing them back to new life. Peacemakers don't jump fences for greener pastures. They do what it takes to put a little more green into the pasture they've been called to.

That's not the course recommended by the world. Peace isn't the world's natural language. It's more comfortable with the vocabulary of separation and estrangement. Most often, its solutions involve the dissolution of relationship rather than reconciliation. Rough

marriage? Divorce. Rotten kids? Write 'em off. Faithless friends? Be faithless in return. Struggling partnership? Grab the goodies and run. For the world, retribution is the rule of relationship—do to others as (or before) they do to you. And the result of following that rule is a string of broken promises, wounded feelings, and lonely people.

But for disciples, the rule of reconciliation reigns. Giving up, letting go, leaving alone is not a disciple's *modus operandi*. Because they are peacemakers, disciples value their relationships enough to deal with problems as they arise—in a way that protects the relationship rather than compromises it.

Want to know what a peacemaker is? A peacemaker is a person who comes to that difficult point in a relationship—when it's time to put up or shut up, stay in or get out—and

> ## TO TRADE OR NOT TO TRADE?
> Americans are trading in their spouses but keeping their automobiles longer. In 1970, the average age of a car on the road was five years. Today it is eight years. Of course, cars have become more reliable and more expensive in the last thirty years—causing us to hang onto our old vehicles. (I was the proud owner of a Chevy Vega in the 1970s. I traded it quickly!)
> **— Consumer Reports**

decides to "make every effort to do what leads to peace."[34] A peacemaker refuses to give up on people they are tied to by blood or commitments or (especially) faith. To the best of their abilities, peacemakers preserve relationships by pursuing peace. If that means forgiving "seventy-seven times,"[35] the peacemaker is willing to go that far. If it requires turning the other cheek, seeking out someone they've offended, returning blessing for curses, enduring a rebuke, making restitution, apologizing—all of these the peacemaker will do, and more.[36]

THE RAREST VIRTUES

*Fools mock at making
    amends for sin,
But goodwill is found among
    the upright.*
                    —Proverbs 14:9

We began this chapter noting that Christians are not particularly known for their willingness to live in peace with each other. Our reputation speaks volumes about the gap that exists between casual professions of faith and real discipleship. Those who merely dabble with Christianity quickly learn to rationalize peace with the world and war with each other. It takes a commitment greater than church attendance to make us more at odds with the world and at peace with God's people.

But many Christians stop their pursuit of Christ before they ever get to peacemaking. Having come so far, they fail to take the final steps that lead to Christlikeness. That's why some people who've confessed their own poverty before God can be so impatient with the failings of their brothers and sisters. It's why people who

have learned to hunger for righteousness can still have so little appetite for peace. Their development as disciples has been arrested—they stop growing before Jesus is through with them.

That's why these last two Beatitudes constitute the rarest of Christian virtues. For every disciple who embraces the peace of Christ and the persecution that's part of being his follower, there are a hundred who have settled for a lesser version of discipleship. One by one, like tired runners in a marathon, Christians drop to the side of the road, content to stop their pursuit of Christ at mourning or meekness or purity of heart. It's a rare disciple indeed who pushes on to a practice of Christlike peace and an endurance of persecution for the sake of Christ.

What a shame. For by the time a Christian is ready for peacemaking, he or she has already been blessed with the virtues that make this peace possible. It takes a disciple who has been broken to self (poverty and mourning) to do whatever is required to mend broken relationships. It takes a disciple who is submitted to God's will (meekness and hunger) to submit to others for the sake of peace. And it takes a disciple who has learned how to treat everyone (with mercy and purity) to know how to treat loved ones when things go wrong.

Peacemaking is the next-to-the-hardest step you'll take in your quest to follow Jesus. But if you can learn to make Christ's peace, the promise is that you will be so much like him, you too will be called a child of God.

AND YOU THOUGHT GOLD WAS RARE

All the world's gold supply could be contained in one sixty-foot cube. That makes it rare and valuable. But the rarest and most expensive naturally occurring element is *Protactinium*, a radioactive and highly toxic metal found only in Zaire. The entire world's stock of this material amounts to 125 grams—less than one-third pound. Yet for all its value, it has no known uses.

— WebElements

TOP TEN . . .

TOP TEN BIBLICAL CHARACTERS WHO DID NOT GIVE PEACE A CHANCE

10. Cain (He just wasn't Abel.)

9. King David (Made the Terminator look tame.)

8. Peter ("Friends, Romans, Malchus, lend me your ear.")

7. King Saul (Gave new meaning to javelin practice.)

6. Samson (Died of fallen arches.)

5. Pontius Pilate ("Gonna wash that man right out of my hands.")

4. Judas Iscariot (The originator of the kiss of death.)

3. Saul of Tarsus (Coat-check boy for the Sanhedrin.)

2. The Four Horsemen of the Apocalypse ("Death and destruction, anyone?")

And the **#1** biblical character who did not give peace a chance:

The Sons of Thunder (*"Now* do we get to call down fire from heaven?")

THE STORY OF...

Mahatma Gandhi

A MAN OF PEACE

You might think it strange that I should single out someone who wasn't a Christian as the greatest peacemaker of our time. But perhaps it requires someone who takes Jesus seriously (though not naming him as Lord) to convict those of us who name Jesus as Lord (but, often, don't take him seriously). The life of Gandhi calls us to think more deeply about the true meaning of Christ's peace.

Mahatma Gandhi was a man of peace. He loved peace. More importantly, he made peace. (Have you seen the movie of his life? Ben Kingsley played Gandhi—a role for which he won the Oscar for Best Actor in 1982. Rent the video and watch a peacemaker in action.)

Gandhi's achievements for the cause of peace were impressive. He managed to establish the independence of India without war or the massing of armed forces. He brought sweeping changes to the social fabric of India, transforming the way the lowest classes were perceived and treated. He found a way (at least for a time) to encourage rival religious factions in India to live at peace with each other.

But it was his commitment to personalizing peace that's most impressive to me. Take, for example, the way he addressed the problem of untouchability. For thousands of years, Indian culture had been divided into castes— levels of social status people were born into and could never escape. This system proved quite acceptable—if you were born into the upper castes (like Gandhi). The further down the social ladder you fell, however, the more difficult and desperate life became.

At the bottom of the ladder were the untouchables (people beneath the caste system, the outcastes). These were people who had no status, who were bereft of rights and privileges. They lived on the edge of survival. They did the dirty work of society—sweeping streets, hauling garbage, carrying sewage, handling dead animals and people. Untouchables were considered completely contaminated and, hence, viewed as untouchable. In practices strangely reminiscent of the Pharisees' treatment of sinners, upper caste Indians were required to purge themselves through ritual washing upon contact (even accidental contact) with untouchables.

Gandhi recognized this system not only as morally outrageous, but as a threat to peace. It encouraged violence against individuals and entire segments of Indian culture. Disdain on one hand and simmering resentments on the other led to a volatile mix of emotions that threatened to boil over into hatred and hostility. How could India demand freedom from British rule, he asked in 1921:

. . . if we desire to keep a fifth of India under perpetual subjection. (Inhuman ourselves, we may not plead before the Throne for deliverance from the inhumanity of others.)

But Gandhi didn't address the untouchability problem with only words or speeches. He didn't fight this battle at the level of ethical and social theories. He took action, very personal action, to deal with untouchability one individual at a time.

For years, Gandhi refused to hire untouchables to do menial household tasks. Instead, he did the untouchable work himself—emptying chamber pots, sweeping floors, and caring for animals. He asked his disciples to contaminate themselves by joining him in such tasks.

When an untouchable family applied for membership in Gandhi's commune, he welcomed them with open arms. They ate at his table and took their turn cooking for the group—thus contaminating everyone associated with the commune. When upper caste financial supporters took offense and withdrew their funding, Gandhi determined to move the commune to the untouchable section of town, where less money would be required. When his own wife objected to the presence of the untouchables, Gandhi listened carefully, appealed to her reasonably, and then begged her not to leave him for insisting that they stay.

He adopted an untouchable as his own daughter. He refused to speak at gatherings where untouchables were not admitted. In 1932, Gandhi declared a fast unto death as a means of protesting the untouchables' lack of representation in the Indian government. Only a quickly arranged compromise at the highest levels of government persuaded him to break his fast. Instead of calling them outcastes or untouchables, Gandhi took to calling them *harijan*—children of God. The name stuck.

There's much here of the peacemaking Jesus spoke of. It's not a passive thing—as if the absence of war is synonymous with peace. It can be an aggressive, demanding quality. It can force nations to their knees and win the day, not by force of arms, but by force of moral authority. It changes people, not by making demands, but through a display of character.

Gandhi was a lifelong student of the Sermon on the Mount. He loved the Beatitudes. I'm profoundly sorry he never yielded his life to Jesus. But, in the end, I'm even sorrier that—in the matter of pursuing peace—he proved himself a more faithful follower of Christ than I often do.

THINKING IT THROUGH

MONDAY

The notion of making peace has a rich history in Scripture. Long before Jesus blessed the peacemakers, it's evident that God valued peace and encouraged its pursuit among his people. Read the following passages and note how fundamental the characteristic of peace is to the nature of God, his Son, and his people.

- The God of peace—Leviticus 26:6; Numbers 6:26; 25:6-12; Proverbs 16:7; Isaiah 60:16-18; Ezekiel 34:24-25; 37:26-28
- The Christ of peace—Isaiah 9:6-7; 53:5; John 14:27; Ephesians 2:14-17; Colossians 1:19-20
- A people of peace—Deuteronomy 20:10-12; Psalm 34:14; Proverbs 12:20; Romans 12:18; 14:19; Ephesians 4:3; Hebrews 12:14

TUESDAY

Like many things in Christian living, peacemaking isn't as simple as it first appears. Just as there are limits to God's patience, so there are limits to his peace. There seems to be a carrot and stick element to God's thinking about this matter. He wants peace. He tries to make peace. But when peace isn't possible, our God isn't afraid to wage war. Read the following passages. What can we learn about God and his peace from these verses?

- Leviticus 26:2-17—An offer of peace or destruction
- Deuteronomy 30:15-20—An offer of blessing or curses
- 1 Samuel 12:14-15—Obedience or rebellion
- Matthew 18:23-35—A king who gives and takes away
- Matthew 22:2-7—A king who invites and punishes

WEDNESDAY

The following statements represent some fairly hard and confrontational words from Jesus. Who are these statements addressed to? What issues are involved? As you read, consider that this is the Prince of Peace talking. What do these statements teach us about the real nature of Christian peace? Are there some people God doesn't ask us to be at peace with?

- Matthew 10:34-38—Choosing between Jesus and those we love
- Matthew 23:15,34—Jesus and the Pharisees
- Luke 13:2-5; John 6:51-66—Hard words for the crowds
- Matthew 16:22-23; John 13:8—Jesus and the conflicted relationship with Peter

THURSDAY

Some practical advice about making peace is found in Paul's letter to the Philippians. Read 2:1-4,14. Write some of your thoughts on the following questions in light of these verses.

- In verse 1, Paul seems to be saying that our ability to make peace is rooted in Christ's attempt to make peace with us — if we have experienced peace with Jesus, then we should be capable of making peace with others. Do you see this?
- What is Paul talking about in verse 2? What would this look like for you?
- What does it mean to "consider others better than yourselves" (verse 3)?
- How do we look out for others and their interests?
- Is it possible to "do everything without complaining or arguing"?

FRIDAY

Review your notes from yesterday. Reread Philippians 2:1-4,14. Now extend what Paul says here to the matter of peacemaking. Would Paul's teachings in these verses help you to practice a more powerful form of peace?

- What would a desire to be like-minded do for your determination to be a peacemaker?
- How would ridding yourself of ambition and conceit, and putting on humility, enhance your effectiveness as a peacemaker?
- Why is the ability to consider the interests of others an important quality for a peacemaker?
- How would refraining from complaining and arguing help you make peace more effectively?

What was the most significant lesson you learned in your study this week?

TALKING IT OVER

TEXT: GENESIS 37:17-20, 26-28; 45:1-7; 50:15-21

WARM-UP:

Have you ever been hurt by someone—really hurt—but found a way to make peace with that person again?

It happens all the time: a spouse is unfaithful, but somehow the marriage is salvaged; a teenager says horrible things, but parents manage to forgive and accept; a friend betrays a confidence, yet the friendship weathers the storm. It's not uncommon for people to make peace when there is every reason for relational war.

Making peace is not an easy thing. It requires our best qualities and efforts. Can you share with the group a time when you made peace with someone who hurt you? Or perhaps a time when you hurt someone and they made peace with you?

Now read Genesis 37:17-20,26-28; 45:1-7; 50:15-21.

DISCUSSION:

This story could have ended in hatred and revenge. Joseph had motive, opportunity, and means to take vengeance on his brothers.

Motive—Did Joseph have good reason to hold a grudge against his brothers? How would most people respond to such treatment?

Opportunity—What brought the brothers to Egypt and to Joseph?

Means—By this time, Joseph was the second most powerful man in Egypt. If he had chosen to avenge himself, what could he have done?

But this story doesn't end in revenge. It ends in tears and forgiveness and kind words. Joseph makes peace with his brothers. The process began long before these men confronted each other.

1. Do you get the impression that Joseph had already forgiven his brothers by the time he actually saw them face to face? What (in the story) would support that conclusion?

2. What perspective on his troubles allowed Joseph to rise above hatred and resentment (see Genesis 50:20)? Might

there have been a time when Joseph dwelt more on the harm his brothers intended than on the good God intended? What changed his mind?

When the confrontation finally occurs and Joseph reveals himself to his brothers, he sends several clear signals that he wants to make peace rather than take revenge.

1. By dismissing his servants (45:1), Joseph ensured privacy. But he also communicated something to his stunned brothers by this action. What?

2. Though Joseph's loud weeping must have perplexed his brothers, it also sent a message. What did Joseph's tears communicate?

3. Look at Joseph's words to his brothers. He asked about his father, he invited them to come closer to him, and he explained their actions as part of God's plan. Do you see how carefully Joseph attempted to put his brothers at ease and communicate his forgiveness?

4. The brothers had a hard time believing. Evidently, they thought Joseph was just biding his time until their father died (see 50:15-21). What did they

do when Jacob died? How, once again, did Joseph make peace with them?

person know you want peace? (You might want to role play this scenario.)

APPLICATION:

1. If you were in Joseph's position, would you make peace or war? Based on your past record, which tendency do you possess?
2. There will always be people who hurt and disappoint us. And we'll always feel a certain measure of resentment and anger about such treatment. Is it possible for us (like Joseph) to change our perspective and, thus, change the way we feel?
3. Often we attempt to make peace with others in order to resolve bad feelings toward them. Joseph's experience suggests that forgiveness comes first and then peacemaking. What do you think?
4. As a group, construct a situation where one of you has the opportunity to make peace with someone who has hurt you. What could you do to communicate your intention to heal the relationship? What could you say that would let the other

COOL DOWN:

Peacemaking is hard work. It requires the best in us. Which of the following qualities are most needed for making peace? Which ones do you need to work on?

- Humility
- Forgiveness
- Wisdom
- Kindness
- Love

   As a group, pray that God will develop these qualities in each of you and then provide you with opportunities to use them in relationships that need healing.

LIVING IT OUT

No Beatitude more clearly shows the intimate connection between all the Beatitudes than the one about peacemaking. You can't practice the seventh Beatitude without learning to practice those that precede it. In fact, it's the faithful practice of the first six Beatitudes that equips you to be a peacemaker.

Consider the following situation: You and a friend have a falling out. There are hurt feelings and hard words between you. Each of you feels wronged. You both retreat into wounded silence and consider whether this relationship is worth the pain.

Enter the peacemaker (that's you). Notice how the intentional practice of the first six Beatitudes provides a step-by-step method for getting to peace. In the list below, I've translated the Beatitudes into relationship language. Think about how a willingness to say these things to an estranged friend might lead to reconciliation and the restoration of a valued relationship.

Poverty of spirit makes it possible to confess, "I was wrong."

Mourning teaches us to say, "I'm sorry; please forgive me."

Meekness causes us to ask, "What is God's will here?"

A hunger for righteousness leads us to affirm, "I want to do what's right."

The quality of mercy drives us to inquire: "What do you need?"

Purity allows us to promise, "I'll be honest with you."

In some ways, peacemaking is little more than the motivation to take what you already know as a disciple and apply it to a particular problem with a particular person. It's a willingness to live out your commitments as a disciple within the context of a specific relationship. It's where the rubber of pious principles meets the road of real life.

Can you think of a past friendship that went sour and stayed sour? How might an application of the Beatitudes to that broken relationship have helped resolve the conflict? What Beatitude rules did you ignore in dealing with that situation?

There's a relationship in your life right now (perhaps a friend, a coworker, or a fellow Christian) that is either unraveling or threatening to do so. It may be that a conflict is brewing or that simple neglect is about to exact its cost. Can you identify that relationship?

Work through the list above, asking yourself, "How could I express these Beatitudes in this specific situation?" Peacemaking begins by imagining a different way of acting—an abnormal solution to a common problem.

Now for the hard question: Do you care enough about this relationship to step in with the Beatitudes and attempt a reconciliation? Can you act like a disciple, even when the issues are up close and personal?

Pick up the phone, call your friend, and set up a time to talk. Go on. Do it now. Don't wait. Peacemaking is a present-tense activity. Procrastinating, putting off until tomorrow, hoping you'll be a peacemaker in the future is only wishful thinking. So screw up your courage, pick up the phone, and call. Your friend is worth it.

The following prayer might help you become a peacemaker.

Father,
I confess that I love myself too much. My first instinct is to protect myself, to defend myself, to take care of myself. And when others threaten me? When they cause me pain or get in my way? Oh, Lord, how quick I am to cut people off and throw away relationships that have become inconvenient.

I know that's not how you act. And how thankful I am. When I fail you, you draw me closer. When I disappoint and hurt you, you're quick to forgive and welcome me home. You always make peace with me. You never throw me away.

Lord, help me to be more like you in this. Teach me to be a peacemaker. Show me how to value others above myself, to care about relationships even when they become difficult. Give me the courage to act like a disciple in the most intimate places of my life—with the people I claim to love. Amen.

IN A WORD

Peacemaking teaches us to say,

"I won't let you go." It's that rare

commitment to live out the Beati-

tudes in the context of a relation-

ship gone sour. It's the instinct to

reconcile—and to trust that Beati-

tude living is the most powerful

means of doing so.

To March Into Hell
for a Heavenly Cause

God will not look you over for medals degrees or diplomas but for scars.
—ELBERT HUBBARD

CHAPTER NINE

"Aaauuurrrgggggghhhhh!" The man on the table writhes in pain until he slumps, half-conscious, into a merciful twilight. A brawny man with shaved head and dull eyes puts down the pliers he has been using and douses his victim with a bucket of dirty water.

The Christian shakes his head and moans. Shattered fingers. Burned flesh. Torn muscle. He's bleeding from mouth and nose and ears. They have been at work on him for hours now. It seems so much longer. Each second crawls past. Though he had vague beliefs about eternity before, now he *knows* eternity exists. Eternity is this room, these men, this agony.

There's a third man in the room—an officer, gaunt and humorless. He stares down at the Christian with neither pity nor malice. Indeed, he seems bored. As if this is all routine. As if he's done this before and will do it again. "Now, once more." He speaks to the ceiling, the words a formality. "Recant your faith. Renounce Christ and all this unpleasantness can cease. Don't let things go any further.

Believe me, it's all downhill from here."

TORTURE CHAMBER
During the Middle Ages, every castle had to have its dungeon (apparently it was part of the ambiance), complete with torture chamber. Most famous example? The Tower of London. Its torture chamber is now a tourist attraction. Take a virtual tour at www.southwark.gov.uk/tourism/fbottom.htm

"Blessed are those who are persecuted because of righteousness, for theirs is the kingdom of heaven."[1]

The man on the table has a dignity that annoys his interrogators. He's suffered well, they grudgingly admit. None of the cursing and invectives which most victims bestow on their tormentors. Just a few mumbled prayers. A scream on occasion when the pain grows too great. The officer thinks to himself, *I prefer it when they rant. I'll take curses over prayer any day.*

The Christian manages a wan smile. He looks through swollen lids and fixes his questioner with the best gaze he can manage. "No, my friend. I will never recant." The voice is still strong. The officer knows instinctively this one will never break. "Do what you will. But hear this. Jesus is Lord. One day, you too will bow down and make that confession."

Freeze frame. Fade to black. "Cut!"

WHAT IS PERSECUTION?

It is infinitely easier to suffer with others than to suffer alone. It is infinitely easier to suffer as a public hero than to suffer apart and in ignominy. It is infinitely easier to suffer physical death than to endure spiritual suffering.

—Dietrich Bonhoeffer

Let's get something straight from the very beginning of this chapter. Persecution is good. It's a sign that Christians are doing something right. Jesus promised that faithful disciples would be persecuted. If we're followers of Jesus, we can't avoid persecution. We don't *want* to avoid it.

We do, however, want to understand it. Frankly, our thinking on the subject is pretty fuzzy. There are so many unanswered questions. What constitutes persecution? Is it physical, or does emotional and relational trauma count? Is it something that only happens long ago or far away or in the movies? Do Christians like you and me experience it here and now in real life? Is religious persecution rare or common?

We can play the torture chamber scene in our heads and agree that it is certainly persecution. But there's something inadequate about *limiting* persecution to physical agonies administered by brutal strangers with the intent of extracting a retraction of faith. What about the pain caused by ridicule and insults and rejection? What about the heartache of watching someone you love laugh at you and turn away when you speak of faith? Doesn't that count?

On the other hand, we don't want to call every spiritual hangnail a satanic plot to destroy our faith. It cheapens persecution to see any inconvenience or temptation or slight as "suffering for the cause of Christ." Losing that parking spot isn't necessarily a sign you have been singled out for suffering—it may just be life.

So, what exactly does Jesus mean when he delivers the final Beatitude?

Does this apply only to the martyrs among us or is there a blessing (and a message) here for all of Christ's followers?

Jesus does place great importance on this matter. He spends more words on the subject of persecution than on any other attribute in the Beatitudes. In fact, where one verse suffices to cover such topics as righteousness and mercy, Jesus takes three verses to talk about persecution. He expands in Matthew 5:11-12 what he starts in 5:10.

"Blessed are you when people insult you, persecute you and falsely say all kinds of evil against you because of me. Rejoice and be glad, because great is your reward in heaven, for in the same way they persecuted the prophets who were before you."

Had Matthew stopped at verse 10, we might be excused for thinking of persecution as whips and chains—and chanting with our children, "Sticks and stones may break my bones, but words will never harm me." But verse 11 makes it clear that words can harm, and that persecution often takes verbal forms. Insults and evil accusations are included in what Jesus calls persecution. People who are ridiculed, lied about, spoken against, and slandered may be just as persecuted as those stretched on a rack.

Once you think about it, this broader definition of persecution makes sense. Jesus was not harmed physically until the final night of his life—but the persecution he endured (particularly from the Pharisees) was constant and longstanding.[2] Their lies about him, their slanders and slights throughout his ministry, were as much persecution as the slaps and beatings they subjected him to during his trial. It didn't require the cross for Jesus to claim he was being persecuted.[3]

That's why we can't limit persecution to dungeons and thumbscrews. When people snub and reject us, when they treat us with contempt, when they abuse us verbally and ridicule our beliefs, we should start to suspect that such treatment might be persecution. When someone says untrue things about you, when you're the focus of gossip and innuendo, when your character is assaulted and your motives are questioned—this, too, can be a form of persecution. There are times when hard words and bitter feelings and verbal attacks aren't just the expressions of unhappy people or obnoxious personalities, but acts of spiritual war intended to inflict suffering on those trying to follow Christ.

When that's the case, disciples shouldn't hesitate to say, "Thank God! I'm being persecuted."

ONE GOOD SNUB DESERVES ANOTHER

My second favorite movie insult: "Your mother was a hamster and your father smelt of elderberries! Now go away, or I shall taunt you a second time!"

— Monty Python and the Holy Grail

SO HERE'S ANOTHER

My favorite movie insult: "To call you stupid would be an insult to stupid people. I've known sheep that could outwit you. I've worn dresses with higher IQs."

— A Fish Called Wanda

WHY WOULD ANYONE PERSECUTE DISCIPLES?

It is remarkable with what Christian fortitude and resignation we can bear the sufferings of other folks.
—JONATHAN SWIFT

Why would anyone want to hurt the kind of person Jesus describes in these Beatitudes? Why should the desire to do right, to mourn sin and submit to God's will, to treat others with compassion and integrity—why would that drive some people to violence? It is perplexing—but nonetheless true—that disciples who take godliness seriously are likely to find themselves facing serious opposition.

Of course, not every Christian who suffers the slings and arrows of others' disdain can claim they are being persecuted for righteousness. Christians can be persecuted for a variety of reasons that really don't count in terms of the kingdom of God. Some of us are merely getting what we deserve.

Take, for instance, those Christians who invite abuse because they've appointed themselves as the morality Gestapo of the world. There are those among us who wouldn't touch a sinner with a ten-foot pole. Modern-day Pharisees who walk around projecting self-righteous judgment shouldn't be surprised if the world reacts violently to them. *Jesus* reacted violently to that kind of sanctimonious arrogance.

Or what about those Christians who have confused oddity with spirituality? When we insist on speaking "religio-babble" (that's God-talk with a liberal amount of King James vernacular sprinkled in), when even conversations with our dentist and mail carrier are frequently punctuated by a loud "Thank ya, Jayeeesssu-ussss!," when both our attitudes and our fashion sense come straight out of the 1950s, we shouldn't expect to be warmly received by the people around us. People in the world neither understand nor appreciate this sort of thing. But it's not because they hate Christ. They just don't like geeks.

The blessing Jesus pronounces here isn't for disciples who've been persecuted for any reason, but for those who have suffered "because of righteousness" (verse 10), or—better yet—"because of me" (verse 11). If others cause us pain because we take discipleship seriously, if we're made to suffer because we want to be like our Lord, if we're ostracized and insulted and maligned for our attempts to live faithfully, Jesus calls that "persecution for the sake of righteousness," and proclaims a blessing on such troubles.

So far, then, we've

GEEK

A person who is overly involved in technology, to the point of sometimes not appearing to be like the rest of us. The term emphasizes singlemindedness and implies social impairment. Historically, a geek was the person in circus sideshows whose role was to bite off chicken heads or perform other bizarre feats. Recent use of the term suggests greater social acceptance and tolerance for geeks. They tend, after all, to make a lot of money.

— whatis.com

learned two things about the kind of persecution Jesus is talking about in this Beatitude. First, it's not necessarily physical. It can include cutting words and strained relationships. Second, it's a persecution brought on by the disciple's love for Jesus and the lifestyle he teaches, not because he or she is socially impaired.

That's the what and the why of persecution. But now comes the hard part. It's time to examine *who* persecutes the disciple. In what follows, I don't mean to downplay the world's eagerness to hurt those who would follow Jesus. Persecution can and does come from unbelievers. But the bad news I must break to you here is that persecution is more frequently an inside job.

WHO PERSECUTES DISCIPLES?

Christians have burnt each other, quite persuaded that all the Apostles would have done as they did.

—LORD BYRON

We tend to think of persecution as something perpetrated by strangers. Whatever form persecution takes—physical or verbal—we don't expect to recognize the faces of our tormentors.

How odd. While there were certainly times through history when secular enemies have persecuted believers, those times have been rare. Most often, the persecutions suffered by God's people originate a little closer to home.

For the real clue to who persecutes righteous people, we need look no further than the Beatitude itself: "In the same way *they* persecuted the prophets who were before you." Who are "they"? Who persecuted the prophets? Jesus answered that very question later in the book of Matthew:

"You [the Pharisees and religious leaders] build tombs for the prophets and decorate the graves

of the righteous. And you say, 'If we had lived in the days of our forefathers, we would not have taken part with them in shedding the blood of the prophets.' So you testify against yourselves that you are the descendants of those who murdered the prophets."[4]

It wasn't the Babylonians or the Ninevites or the Egyptians or the Philistines who persecuted the prophets. It wasn't strangers or the high priests of pagan religions who ridiculed, slandered, imprisoned, and sometimes killed God's spokesmen. It was the prophets' own compatriots, their neighbors, members of their families, people who bowed down to the same God and worshiped at the same temple. Jeremiah suffered at the hands of his fellow prophets, his king, and his neighbors—priests who claimed to serve Yahweh.[5] Moses faced more painful opposition from his fellow Israelites (and even from his own brother and sister) than from Pharaoh and the Egyptians. Righteous Job was tormented by men who claimed to be his friends. Hosea knew his persecutor intimately—this prophet's wife caused him more anguish and heartbreak than the Assyrians ever did.

Come to think of it, the same thing is true of Jesus. It wasn't Caesar and his representatives who caused Jesus the most problems. It wasn't pagan idol worshipers and polytheists. His betrayer was one of his own disciples. His persecutors were his own countrymen, his co-religionists, those who ostensibly shared his commitment to Yahweh. The real enemies of Jesus were dressed like him, spoke his language, said the same prayers, attended the same worship assemblies, and read the same Scriptures. These weren't aliens from another religious planet. They were Jesus' neighbors and peers. Jesus knew them by name. He recognized their faces.[6]

As hard as it is to accept, the persecution disciples are called to endure often will be at the hands of people we know, people we worship with, people who also claim to be religious. The person behind the tormenter's mask may well be someone we thought was a friend. The source of that slanderous remark or gossipy tidbit making the rounds at your expense frequently will turn out to be someone you trusted, someone you loved, someone you thought was following Jesus.

It's not strangers, hell-bent on destroying the faith, we should fear most. It's those people we break bread with. They're the ones most likely to break our hearts.

YOUR ENEMIES WILL BE MEMBERS OF YOUR HOUSEHOLD
What mean and cruel things men do for the love of God.
—Somerset Maugham

This isn't an invitation to paranoia. I'm not encouraging you to keep a suspicious eye on your fellow church member nor warning you against intimate relationships because they may wound you later. What I am saying is that serious commitment to Christ cuts not just between believers and unbelievers—the church and the world—but between those who hunger to be like Christ and those who see casual Christianity as good enough.

Christianity has been around long enough now to have been thoroughly domesticated. For two thousand years, we've pruned and trimmed and snipped at it—excising all of the prickly parts so we can embrace the faith without any pain. For many, the Christ who confronts has been traded for a Christianity that always comforts. The call to follow has been supplanted by the call to church. Transformation has been set aside in favor of tradition and ritual. The vital, shattering, life-changing religion of Jesus has been institutionalized . . . sanitized . . . sterilized.

The prime directive for many churches and their members has become non-interference in the placid practice of a tame religion. "Don't rock the boat. Let sleeping Christians lie. Go through the motions. Do the bare minimum. Discourage zeal in any form. Blessed are the innocuous."

The Beatitudes (and the disciples who take them seriously) threaten that kind of Christianity. They won't allow the status quo. They won't permit tranquility and navel-gazing. They're the stuff of personal and institutional revolution. They turn everything they touch upside-down. They refuse to be church-broken.

Had Jesus come today, it wouldn't have been the Pharisees who crucified him. It would have been us! We

> ## THE PRIME DIRECTIVE
> According to Star Fleet Regulations, the Prime Directive reads: "As the right of each sentient species to live in accordance with its normal cultural evolution is considered sacred, no Star Fleet personnel may interfere with the healthy development of alien life and culture."
> — www.startrek.com

would have found Jesus and his hard words just as threatening, just as frightening, as did the religious leaders of his own day. To protect the "temple," to quiet the turmoil, to maintain our perks and our places,[7] we'd be just as likely to rid ourselves of this troublemaker as they were.

How can I say such a thing? By noting how we deal with people who dare to be Christlike today. Nothing will provoke the ire of fellow church members quite so much as trying to put the Beatitudes into practice. Everything about these teachings touches something sensitive in the merely religious. We don't want poverty, we want plenty. We don't want tears, we want laughter. Who needs hunger when you can be self-satisfied? Why be merciful when it's so inconvenient? There have always been Christians highly motivated to practice a Christianity that

doesn't involve Christ.

That's why disciples who take the Beatitudes seriously should expect to be persecuted. But not by faceless strangers plying their torturous trade in dungeon cells. Rather, that persecution most likely will come from brothers and sisters who are afraid of the water and don't want you rocking their spiritual boat.

Get serious about confession, and watch how nervous the Christians around you become. Pursue heartfelt penitence, and notice fellow believers starting to wonder if it's catching. Determine to submit every area of your life to God's will, and listen to other Christians whisper, "Fanatic!" Develop a passion for the holy, and observe believing friends rolling their eyes and shaking their heads. Practice indiscriminate mercy, and discover how it threatens other Christians' checkbooks and Day Timers. Determine to live honestly and with complete

> ## FANATIC
> The Latin word for "temple" was fanum. Individuals who went into trances or received revelations in the temple were called fanatici. In time, the word was used to label any person who acted frantic, frenzied, or insane. In modern English usage, fanatic is applied to those who are excessively enthusiastic or extreme. The word fan is probably derived from fanatic.
> —Merriam-Webster Word Histories

integrity, and see how frantically those around you grab for their fig leaves. Try your best to make peace, and listen to a chorus of recrimination rising from the pews.

The Beatitudes are bewildering to the secular world. When secular people persecute, they do so out of ignorance. But the Beatitudes are *threatening* to church members who would rather leave well-enough alone. You have to speak the Christian language to understand just how dangerous these statements are. Reacting to that threat, addressing that danger, the merely religious will persecute disciples who attempt to embody the Beatitudes. Only they do so not out of ignorance but out of fear, scared to death that a Beatitude kind of discipleship is a comment on and criticism of the tepid Christianity they've chosen to practice.

CROSSING THE LINE

Everyone who wants to live a godly life in Christ Jesus will be persecuted....[8]

We practice the Beatitudes at our own risk. Take the spiritual steps Jesus recommends in these statements, listen and act upon his instructions for becoming the kind of disciple he wants you to be, and there will be people you know and love—church members, family members, Christian friends—who'll turn on you and tell you to knock it off.

They usually begin with ridicule. They'll compare your former apathy with your newfound zeal, and laugh off as a passing phase your attempts to follow Jesus. They'll deride your efforts to take Christ's statements at face value ("Those are beautiful words, but nobody tries to *live* like that!"). They'll point out every one of your missteps and jump on every inconsistency. You'll become the butt of their jokes and the object of their derision. The first cost of discipleship is that no one takes you seriously.

THE DANGERS OF BEING DIFFERENT
Turkeys will peck to death members of the flock that are noticeably different. This strange behavior may represent an instinct to preserve the species.
—North Carolina State University

If ridicule fails, they'll try insults. They'll question your motives, doubt your intelligence, and dispute your sincerity. They'll accuse you of arrogance for pursuing a different spiritual path than the one they've chosen. They'll hurl at you the charge of being holier-than-us. Instead of laughing at your mistakes (and there will be plenty to laugh at), they'll search for fresh failures to use for poking holes in your renewed enthusiasm for Christ.

If insults don't dissuade you, they will slander and malign you. You'll be labeled as fanatical and dangerous. Others will be warned that you constitute a threat to the church's peace, that you're a troublemaker stirring up unnecessary aggravations. It will be said that underlying your zeal is a dark and secret sin—that it's not the love of Christ but a killing guilt that motivates your efforts. You'll be accused of despising your religious heritage and denigrating the religious devotion of those around you. You'll become the object of peoples' suspicions and gossip and innuendo.

When slander doesn't bring you to your senses, they'll try rejection. Friendships will suffer, fellowship will be broken, relationships will become strained. People will withhold their affections in an attempt to discipline you back into the somnolent fold. You'll be made to feel like an outsider whose viewpoints are unappreciated and whose input is unwelcome. You'll become a stranger to the very people who once were your home.

If still you persist in your headlong pursuit of Christ, there are many of your religious compatriots who'll decide (with a sigh) that you should be punished. They'll reprimand you publicly, loudly calling evil what you know to be good. They'll strip you of responsibilities in the church and forbid you to poison other minds with your heresy. You'll be strung up on verbal racks and left to twist in the wind. They'll brutalize you in an attempt to shut you up, cool you off, calm you down.

And if, in the end, even punishment doesn't make you conform, they'll determine to destroy you. Oh, they won't be able to do it with sword or stake. There are laws against that sort of thing nowadays — the merely religious are meticulous about observing laws. But there's more than one way to crucify a disciple. They can assassinate your character. They can kill your reputation. They can murder your ministry. And they will, if that's what it takes.

I know these are hard words. I realize the notion that persecution is more likely to come from fellow believers than from godless sinners is hard to swallow.

Perhaps you're telling yourself, "Church people wouldn't act like this! Christians wouldn't treat me this way." I can only respond with Jesus' words:

"Remember the words I spoke to you: 'No servant is greater than his master.' If they persecuted me, they will persecute you also." [9]

Here's that "they" again. Perhaps Jesus was thinking here only of the Roman soldiers who would nail him to the cross. But I doubt it. I imagine he had most clearly in mind the members of his own religious family who, in the end, would rather kill than submit to him. The escalation of persecution I traced above (from ridicule to insult to slander to rejection to punishment to destruction) is precisely the pattern of persecution employed by the Pharisees and religious authorities in dealing

TWISTING IN THE WIND

In the ancient world, death was not sufficient punishment! They had to add insult to fatal injury. The bodies of hanging victims were often left to "twist in the wind." The phrase today refers to any treatment that isn't just injurious, but humiliating.

—*Dictionary of Phrase and Fable*

with Jesus. It's the exact pattern followed by the Jewish authorities and Christian Judaizers in the early church for dealing with Paul. It's the pattern adopted in every age by a moribund church as it deals with people who attempt to reform and revive it. It's most certainly the pattern that will be used on you if you're reckless enough to take these Beatitudes seriously.

If certain religious people, in the name of God and by the authority of the church, could persecute Jesus to the death; if they could hound Paul all over the Mediterranean world and undermine his work at every opportunity; if they could burn fellow Christians at the stake and torture innocent disciples for pursuing holiness, don't think for a moment they will shrink from doing whatever is necessary to keep you at a safe distance from Christ and his Beatitudes.

The question for disciples

is not whether we'll be persecuted, but how we'll respond to that persecution. It seems there are four options for us when we suffer for righteousness. We can back down and permit the persecutors to have their way. We can hang on, hoping to outlast them. We can retaliate and make them pay for the pain they are causing. Or we can take the final option.

REJOICE AND BE GLAD

Persecution is never fun. The agonies of insult and rejection are no laughing matter. When Jesus tells us to "rejoice and be glad" when persecuted, he's not trying to trivialize our pain or recommend an absurd response to a serious situation.

What he does tell us is that persecution is both a *validation* and an *opportunity*. Christians can rejoice when

persecuted because such suffering says something about their character and provides a chance for that character to shine most brightly.

Persecution is the litmus test of Christian character. The more you embody the virtues described in the Beatitudes, the more likely it is that someone around you will see red. I say that hesitantly, reminding you that not every pain we suffer is the result of "persecution for righteousness." Spiritual wisdom and maturity are required to distinguish between suffering caused by our own sin or stupidity and that which results from our sincere attempts to become Christlike.

But pain isn't always a sign that you're doing something wrong. There are times when persecution is the ultimate vindication of how very right you have been. The prophets suffered because they were so completely yielded to the will of God. Jesus endured his greatest agonies while accomplishing his holiest work. The more Paul shed himself and put on Christ, the less some people liked it. There are times when nothing authenticates our walk with Jesus like a healthy dose of painful opposition.

That's why we can "rejoice and be glad" when we're persecuted. Suffering is one way God can stamp his approval on our lives. When Satan pulls out all the big guns in his considerable arsenal and aims them at us, when he unleashes his demons to spit their venom, it can only mean he sees something in our lives that he hates and wants to destroy. The only thing in my failed life that Satan could possibly object to is Christ, alive and growing in me. When he persecutes me, I know it's because I look a little more like Jesus, smell a little more like Jesus, act a little more like Jesus, am a little more like Jesus. Now that's cause for celebration!

Persecution, however, is more than vindication—it is also *opportunity*. We have a chance, in the midst of persecution, to demonstrate that the character changes God has affected in us are not just skin deep. They cannot be rubbed off with a little suffering.

The reason people persecute Christians is to get them to cease and desist. "Stop acting like that! Quit behaving in those ways! Knock off that Jesus stuff." When we decline to be persuaded, Satan employs persecution. He'll try to force what he cannot seduce. When Satan decides to turn up the heat, pain (like a fire) reduces us to core values. What kind of people are we when we're hurting?

The opportunity in persecution involves a demonstration of Beatitude living in the midst of suffering. If we can confess our spiritual poverty rather than bemoan the moral deficiencies of our persecutors, if we can mourn our own sins rather than those of the people who oppose us, if we can stay submitted to God when the temptation is to submit to our sufferings, if we can demonstrate a passion for righteousness that will not be quenched by pain and troubles, if we can show mercy even to our enemies, if we can live with integrity among those who do not, if we can attempt to build bridges to people who are equally intent on building walls— we will become living proof that good really does overcome evil, that life can swallow up death, and that right is more powerful than might.

The ability to suffer without retaliation, to bless those who curse you, to love your enemies, to do good to those who treat you cruelly—this is the ultimate virtue. To "keep your head when all about you are losing theirs and blaming it on you" (to use Rudyard Kipling's memorable line) is the greatest and highest expression of Christlike character. To watch those you love turn against you, and to keep loving them.

To hear people you trust slander and malign you, and to respond with graciousness. To see your credibility undermined and your witness ridiculed, yet to refuse revenge, trusting yourself instead to God. When you can respond to persecution in these ways, you embody the character Jesus wants to build in his disciples.

And you can rejoice and be glad. For you are in good company. Many a godly man and woman have suffered for the cause of righteousness. And many have found in the crucible of pain the courage to demonstrate a Christlike character. If you're one of their number, count yourself blessed. The kingdom of heaven belongs to people like you.

TOP TEN . . . .

TOP TEN INDICATORS YOU MAY BE SUFFERING FOR SELF-RIGHTEOUSNESS RATHER THAN RIGHTEOUSNESS

10. Your personal testimony is always about the power of rigorous fasting, sacrificial giving, and lengthy public prayers.

9. You never leave home without your driver's license, Social Security card, and a miniature copy of your baptismal certificate.

8. You paint a halo on your driver's side door for every convert you make.

7. You sincerely believe you could have beaten out John for "Best-Loved Apostle."

6. You can't figure out why people dislike you, when you know yourself to be so lovable.

5. You put yourself to sleep each night by counting your virtues. ("One thousand one, one thousand two. . . .")

4. Someone keeps writing graffiti on your "Be like me or burn eternally" billboard.

3. Your basic approach to evangelism is, "I said it. That settles it. Any questions?"

2. Your quartet was forced to forfeit the "Praise Trophy" at the National Worship Competition when you publicly denounced the soprano as ineligible.

And the **#1** indicator you may be suffering for self-righteousness rather than righteousness:

You embarrass your children when you insist on singing, "Happy birthday to thee."

THE STORY OF . . .

Billy Graham

TURNING THE OTHER CHEEK

William Franklin Graham is the closest thing the modern world has to an evangelistic icon. For five decades, he's preached to massive audiences and ministered to those in high office. While other famous evangelists have taken very public falls, Graham has conducted himself in an honorable and Christlike manner. Now, as many reflect on fifty years of public ministry, it's rare to hear anything but praise and admiration for the man and his ministry.

But Billy Graham hasn't always escaped criticism and opponents. Especially in the early years, reporters felt free to print scathing evaluations of his work and beliefs. There have been occasions when unbelievers

caused him suffering for preaching the gospel. But, in reading his autobiography, *Just As I Am*, what strikes you is how often opposition and criticism came from Graham's *fellow believers*.

Graham was introduced to this sad fact of life early in his ministry. Members of his first congregation in Western Springs, Illinois, complained about his absences for evangelistic meetings and criticized the kind of people he was bringing into the church. The young Graham struggled to understand how his own brothers and sisters could be so harsh.

Every speaker has experienced the occasional heckler calling out comments and attempting to divert attention to himself. But, while preaching in England, Graham was heckled by a fellow minister, who stood up in the middle of his sermon and proclaimed it all heresy. He shouted his objections

until, finally, this "man of God" had to be escorted bodily from the church. During another meeting (this time in Pennsylvania), several people interrupted Graham's sermon to condemn him for fellowshipping with people they considered too liberal.

Graham has always been required to deal with his clergy critics—ministers who not only saw fault in Graham but voiced their concerns to anyone who'd listen. They accused him of being an entertainer, undermining commitment to the local church (although one of Graham's most cherished goals is just the opposite), associating with known sinners, and preaching a watered-down gospel. They publicly questioned his motives, his integrity, his intelligence, and his beliefs. They raised eyebrows over his finances and deliberately misquoted his remarks.

Billy Graham has taken deliberate steps to keep his behavior above reproach. The financial dealings of his ministry are audited annually and the results made public. He refuses to meet alone with women—even in public places—to avoid any hint of sexual impropriety. But some of his fellow pastors seem to delight in reproaching him anyway. Graham confesses that nothing hurts quite so badly as this sort of treatment from this group of people.

Through it all, Graham has managed to turn the other cheek. You don't hear any notes of bitterness or anger in his autobiography. Just the opposite. Graham is gentle with his opponents and apologizes for reactions which—at the time—were not as gentle as he now might wish. When telling of some difficult moment or a distressing confrontation, he reserves criticism for his own behavior rather than focusing on the flaws of his detractors. Where you or I might be defensive, Graham has learned to suffer quietly and trust God to set the record straight.

To the best of my knowledge, Graham has never lost a drop of his own blood for the cause of Christ. He's never been beaten or stoned. He hasn't had his property confiscated or his family arrested.

But he has known persecution. He has suffered for daring to speak up for God. People—even some of God's people—have caused him pain for being a prophet. But Billy Graham can rejoice in this. It's God's vindication that he's doing something right. And it's his opportunity to show how a man of God conducts himself when the going gets tough.

THINKING IT THROUGH

MONDAY

Jesus pointed to the prophets as examples of people who suffered (and even died) for daring to speak up for God. Perhaps it would be useful to refresh our memories of who these people were, how they suffered, and what they did to deserve persecution.

- Moses was called a prophet (Deuteronomy 34:10)—Numbers 12:1-2; 14:1-4; 16:1-3,41-45
- Elijah—1 Kings 19:1-4
- Ezekiel—Ezekiel 2:3-8
- Prophets in general—Hosea 9:7-8; Matthew 21:29-35,37; Acts 7:52; James 5:10

TUESDAY

I mentioned in this chapter that "Jesus was not harmed physically until the last night of his life, but the persecution he endured was constant and longstanding." Let's look at some of the ways Jesus suffered for the sake of the kingdom (particularly at the hands and tongues of religious leaders). Do the following incidents qualify as persecution?

- Matthew 12:1-14,22-24; 13:53-57; 15:1-3; 22:15-22
- Mark 3:1-6; 8:11-12; 14:53-65
- Luke 7:36-39,44-47; 9:51-53; 11:53-54; 13:10-14; 14:1-6; 19:37-44
- John 5:10-16; 6:41-43, 60-66; 7:1-13; 8:12-13, 48-53; 10:19-20

WEDNESDAY

Paul tells Timothy that "everyone who wants to live a godly life in Christ Jesus will be persecuted" (2 Timothy 3:12). That was certainly true of first-century Christians. Look at the following passages and ask yourself these questions: (1) What is said in this passage about persecution? (2) Are there any hints about the form persecution takes? (3) Who is doing the persecuting?

- Acts 9:4-5 (In what way was Paul persecuting Jesus?)
- Acts 12:1-4; 13:50; 26:9-11
- 1 Corinthians 4:12-13
- Hebrews 10:32-36
- 1 Peter 3:9,13-16; 4:12-14

THURSDAY

The Bible doesn't simply warn of persecution or give examples of people who suffered for the kingdom. It recommends a certain course of action for Christians when they're persecuted—an ideal for Christians to reach for as they endure insults, slanders, and even physical suffering. List the recommendations you read in the following verses and think of ways to put these ideals into practice.

- Luke 6:22-23,27-31
- Romans 5:3-5; 12:14
- 1 Corinthians 4:12-13
- 2 Corinthians 12:10
- 2 Thessalonians 1:4-6
- 2 Timothy 2:3; 4:5
- Hebrews 12:1-4
- James 1:2-4
- 1 Peter 2:21-23; 3:9-14; 4:12-16

FRIDAY

The book of Revelation was written to Christians facing persecution. Some, no doubt, were being ridiculed and slandered. Many, however, faced physical persecution for claiming Jesus as Lord. Notice some of the themes that come up in this book. Comment in your notes on how these ideas apply to your life today.

- John writes to prepare fellow Christians to stand firm in the difficult days ahead—Revelation 1:9; 2:1-3,8-13; 3:4-12.
- He describes a war between the forces of God and those of Satan. In wars, people get hurt, they suffer, they are persecuted—Revelation 12:7-11; 13:5-10; 17:3-6.
- Several times in Revelation "martyrs" or "witnesses" are mentioned. It's difficult (in a book so full of symbolic language) to know whether John was referring to people who actually gave their lives for the faith or to Christians who didn't deny the faith even when slandered and abused. Whoever they are, they're considered special people—Revelation 6:9-11; 7:9-17; 11:7-12; 20:4-6.

- John's advice is consistent throughout: "This calls for patient endurance and faithfulness"—Revelation 13:10; 14:12.

What was the most significant lesson you learned in your study this week?

TALKING IT OVER

TEXT: JEREMIAH 11:21-23; 18:18; 20:1-2,7-10; 26:7-11; 38:2-6

WARM-UP:

Most Christians in modern America don't expect to be tortured for their faith. Ridiculed perhaps. Resented and rejected maybe. But not tortured.

Go around the group and ask the following questions: What is persecution? Does being ridiculed for your faith count? Can you share with the group an occasion when you spoke up as a Christian and were shot down by the people around you? Is that persecution? Who do we expect to persecute us? Do we usually think in terms of strangers or enemies of the faith to be the ones who cause suffering for the sake of the Lord?

With this in mind, have members of the group turn to one of the following passages, read it aloud, and then keep the Bible open at that passage for further study: Jeremiah 11:21-23; 18:18; 20:1-2,7-10; 26:7-11; 38:2-6.

DISCUSSION:

1. Why did Jeremiah suffer persecution? What reasons did his persecutors give for abusing him? (Look at your texts for answers.) Would you call what Jeremiah endured "persecution for the sake of righteousness"?
2. Think a little more carefully about the kind of persecution Jeremiah suffered. Some of it was very physical. List some of the ways Jeremiah was made to suffer physically.
3. Some of it, however, was psychological. It involved ridicule, slander, and rejection. Look at your texts again for evidence of this kind of persecution. Does this kind of abuse really qualify as "persecution"?
4. Think also about who persecuted Jeremiah. The enemies of Israel at the time were the Babylonians. Their army was threatening to destroy Jerusalem. But were these the people who mistreated the prophet?
5. Who beat Jeremiah and threw him in prison and told lies about him?
6. Notice 11:21. A group of men from Anathoth plotted to shut

Jeremiah up by killing him. Now look at Jeremiah 1:1. What was Jeremiah's home town? What does this imply?
7. Talk a little about Jeremiah's courage (or stubbornness!). Did persecution persuade him to be quiet? What do you think about a man who could take this kind of abuse and still keep speaking for God?

APPLICATION:

1. Why do we suffer persecution today? Most of the time, when we are persecuted, is it because:
   - we speak up for Christian viewpoints?
   - we are different?
   - we are irrelevant?
   - or we are obnoxious?

   Is it possible that we are abused on occasion for something other than our righteousness?
2. As the experience of Jeremiah indicates, persecution can take many forms. What kind of physical persecutions are modern Christians likely to encounter? What kind of psychological persecutions do we endure? (Give some

examples.) Are ridicule and rejection as much forms of persecution as beatings?

3. Who is most likely to persecute us? It was Jeremiah's own countrymen, his fellow prophets, his friends and neighbors who caused him the most pain. What if the same is true for us? Name some situations in which the following groups could "persecute us for righteousness": family members, friends, members of our church.

COOL DOWN:
How are you going to respond to persecution? Will it shut you up, slow you down, or increase your determination? What would it look like for you to "rejoice and be glad" in the midst of persecution?

As a group, pray that God will make his word "like a fire" in your hearts so that, even in persecution, you "cannot hold it in."

LIVING IT OUT

Rudyard Kipling's famous poem "If" isn't about persecution or suffering or even about faith. It has to do with honor and character and what it means to be an "English gentleman." Yet the wise advice given in this poem provides a pointed and practical guide for Christians concerned with conducting themselves well in the face of opposition.

I have selected some lines from the poem for you to consider and use in shaping your own response to slander, lies, ridicule, and other forms of religious persecution.

The first line of Kipling's poem addresses a key issue for Christians: Will our behavior be determined by how we are treated or does Jesus empower us to act better than that? Too often, we give ourselves permission (especially in difficult or unfair circumstances) to act at the level of those around us.

If you can keep your head
    when all about you
Are losing theirs and blaming
    it on you.

But Jesus (and Kipling) suggests that it's possible to rise above the littleness of others, to find a higher standard of behavior. We can bless when cursed. We can be kind to those who are cruel. We can "keep our heads" in spite of the fact that others are giving way to anger and fear. Memorizing and quoting Kipling's line to yourself at difficult moments may help you keep your head.

If you can wait and not be
    tired by waiting,
Or, being lied about,
    don't deal in lies,
Or, being hated, don't give
    way to hating,
And yet don't look too good,
    nor talk too wise;

How do we respond to "being lied about" or "being hated"? Again, the temptation is to respond in kind. But the call of Christ means that certain tactics are out of bounds for Christians. No matter how difficult the circumstances, we simply do not "deal in lies" or "give way to hate." If persecution becomes an excuse to do wrong, what has been gained?

Where is the victory in that?

Kipling suggests something even more subtle, however. It's not enough to rise above the poor behavior of others. We must do so without pride or superiority ("don't look too good, or talk too wise"). These are hard words to hear. If we can act better than others, we ought to be able to crow about it a little! We want to draw attention to our sterling character and stiff upper lip. Not so, says Kipling (and Jesus). Christians must suffer well. But they must also suffer quietly. It is enough for God to know our hearts and our courage.

If you can bear to hear the
    truth you've spoken
Twisted by knaves to make a
    trap for fools,
Or watch the things you gave
    your life to broken,
And stoop and build 'em up
    with wornout tools.

Persecutors don't know how to build—only how to tear down. And what they want to tear down most is your character, your credibility, the kingdom work you've given your life to. How do you respond to the spiritual vandals in your life? To the hecklers and detractors and cynics?

Jesus knew what it meant to have his words twisted and used against him. He faced his share of kingdom vandals. Yet he confronted his persecutors with tranquility. He refused to allow their hatred and destructiveness to affect his own behavior. He listened to their lies and forgave. He watched them tear down and stooped to build again. Can we do that? Are we that strong?

You might want to memorize these lines of Kipling's poem. The next time you find yourself in a situation where someone is saying ugly things or questioning your motives or ridiculing your faith, repeat these lines to yourself. They may remind you that persecution is an opportunity to let Christian character shine even when times are hard.

The following prayer might prepare you for your next encounter with persecution:

Father,
You have promised that those who love you will experience persecution. If there were people who hated your Son, there will be people who hate me also.
I don't ask to avoid those people, Lord, or the pain they may cause me. But I do ask that you:
- *give me wisdom—to recognize persecution when it happens.*
- *give me courage—to endure whatever pain I'm called to face.*
- *give me strength—to react in Christlike ways even when I'm hurting.*
Most of all, my Lord, give me joy—to see persecution as a sign of your favor and a chance to join your Son in his sufferings. Amen.

IN A WORD

Persecution teaches us to say, **"I will follow Jesus—regardless."** When faced with ridicule or rejection—even by those we know and love—our determination is to rejoice, endure, and demonstrate the character of Jesus.

PROMISES, Promises

n the closing days of World War II, Allied bombings of the munitions factories around Essen, Germany, became more frequent and fierce. When the air raid sirens sounded, armed guards would rush to bomb shelters, leaving the slave laborers (often Jewish and female) to huddle in the rubble and take their chances.

On March 11, 1945, at the height of an endless bombardment, Elizabeth Roth and five companions decided to make their escape. They crept to the barbed wire surrounding the factory where they worked, crawled through a gap, and made their way across an empty field to a hill overlooking the town where they hoped to find a hiding place.

There, on the verge of freedom, one of the girls lost her nerve. Quietly, she turned back, recrossed the field, crawled back through the wire, and returned to the wreckage of the factory. The next day, along with five hundred other female workers, she was loaded onto a train and sent to Buchenwald and the gas chambers.

In recounting this story, William Manchester remarks,

It is a common phenomenon among escapees; the known, however ghastly, seems preferable to the unknown.[1]

"Who would do such a thing?" you might ask. "What sane person would make such a tragic decision?" The answer is, "We would."

LOOKING OVER THE PROMISED LAND

Like Elizabeth and her friends, we know what it's like to be imprisoned in a broken world. We've been there, living amid the wreckage, cowering under the consequences of our own failure and surrounded by shattered lives, ruined relationships, and failed hopes.

Then, one day, Jesus comes and offers a means of escape. He takes us by the hand and leads us away from our old lives and habits. Over the wreckage and through the barriers and across the barren fields that separate us from God, Jesus guides us to a place overlooking the possibility of shelter and deliverance. From a high hill, we're given a glimpse of the life God.

We sit on that mountainside with Jesus, gazing at the Beatitudes and thinking what life could be like if we walked his way. You can almost hear the wheels turning in the minds of our fellow escapees. "Is this possible? Can you teach an old dog like me new tricks? Maybe I should just go back to what I know."

The dangers of the unfamiliar, the risks of that uncharted territory, sink in like the cold. A man behind us stands and turns down the mountain, leaving Jesus and his challenging Beatitudes. A woman to our right jumps to her feet and follows the man. Several others make their regretful way back to their old lives and comfortable ways and fatal habits.

We feel the pull to join them. For every Beatitude, there is a "Yes, but . . ." begging to be raised. A bevy of rationalizations and excuses flit through our minds. The fear of following Jesus into the unknown weighs heavily on us all. When it comes to matters of the Spirit, we're all afraid of heights.

This book has been a survey of the kind of living Jesus proposes for his disciples. I hope that through it you've seen something of the possibilities in Beatitude living. But I suspect some of us are still hesitant to march down the hill and take up residence in the Beatitudes. The unknown is just too frightening. Leaving the familiar behind, even when the familiar is dysfunctional, is a difficult thing.

So, what's to keep us from losing our nerve? What can persuade us not to let go of the hand that has brought us this far? How can we avoid rushing back to the old habits, which have served us so long, if not so well?

IT'S THE PROMISES, STUPID!

There are two parts to any self-respecting Beatitude.

Blessed are the poor in spirit (trait), for theirs is the kingdom of heaven (promise).

This structure is followed rigorously in the eight Beatitudes of Matthew 5:3-10. And it can be found in other places through the Bible.[2] It's the natural shape for a Beatitude to take—a recommended behavior followed by an attractive promise.

I anticipate one criticism of this book will be that too much emphasis has been placed on the first part of the Beatitudes and too little on the last. I've focused on the *traits* Jesus describes rather than the *promises* he pronounces. "The Beatitudes are meant to congratulate disciples and teach them the benefits of following Jesus," someone might say. "You've taken a list of spiritual blessings and turned them into a list of spiritual chores."

Maybe. I *have* gone to great lengths to discuss meekness and hunger and purity, and spent relatively little time talking about "inheriting the earth" and being "satisfied" and "seeing God." I do understand the Beatitudes as *prescriptive* ("This is how you should live") rather than as *congratulatory* ("My compliments on how you're already living").

The only word I will offer in defense is that sometimes it takes one extreme to counterbalance another. We come to these Beatitudes eager to hear the blessings and loathe to hear

any demand. We're all ears when God makes promises and stone deaf when he talks of expectations. We want unconditional gifts, blessings without strings, promises that make no demands.

Our natural tendency is to suck the benefits from the Beatitudes and spit out the lifestyle. We put discipleship on the installment plan—enjoying all the blessings now while postponing the transformation to later. Much later.

That's why I have focused on the character traits of discipleship rather than the promises attached to them. *Our* most pressing business is to yield ourselves to the lifestyle Jesus commends. *God's* business is to bless that kind of living.

But, having said that, the promises are included in the Beatitudes for a reason. They're important, even necessary, parts of these statements. And I suspect they're vital because only the promises can persuade us to put the Beatitudes into action. They're God's inducement to risk the

unknown. They're the means God employs to lure us away from our old lives and encourage us to adopt a new standard of living. In the end, only the promises can keep us from turning back to the familiar and, instead, impel us headlong into a brave new world.

Here, then, are the promises God makes to those who follow his instructions for being a disciple. These are the treasures at the end of the search. You judge whether they justify the risk of living so close to the spiritual edge.

THE HEAVENLY JACKPOT

Cutting to the chase—Jesus promises heaven and earth to those who take the Beatitudes seriously. Here's the grand prize, the bonanza, the buried treasure. The Beatitudes mark the spot where those who want it all must dig.

It's a question of motivation. How can Jesus inspire us to risk the Beatitude lifestyle? He tells us that the rewards are worth the gamble.

To begin, Jesus bookends the Beatitudes with a phrase that—if only we understood it—would take our breath away. The first and eighth Beatitude make the incredible promise:

. . . for theirs is the kingdom of heaven.

Start with poverty of spirit, move step by step through the rest of the Beatitudes, mature to the point that even persecution can't dissuade you from being a disciple—and Jesus promises the kingdom of heaven will be yours.

The "kingdom" was Jesus' shorthand for the presence of God, the reign of God, the realm of God. The kingdom is where God is and where God rules. That's why Jesus talked about it so much (fifty times in Matthew's gospel alone). He urged people to enter the kingdom, to sacrifice everything to possess the kingdom, to do whatever was required to force their way into the kingdom.[3] Being "in" the kingdom is to

live in God, to enjoy his favor and his blessings, to know at last the true meaning of life.

As you sit on the brow of life and contemplate a decision to live out the Beatitudes, I want you to know that—in promising the kingdom of heaven—Jesus is betting the farm. To have the kingdom is to have it all. This, in one phrase, is everything Jesus cares about. It's what he lived and died for.

Jesus invites us to join him in the Beatitudes. He promises that in them are the limitless riches and boundless blessings that flow from living in the presence of God. Sounds like an offer we can't refuse.

But Jesus isn't done.

Looking through all the treasures kingdom people enjoy, Jesus picks out a few of the best to highlight in the remainder of the Beatitudes. He can't name all the blessings available to those who have the courage to live with the Beatitudes, but he can call our attention to those that glitter most brightly.

Like *comfort*. It may not sound like much at first. Nothing that an old leather chair or a warm sweater can't provide. But if you think about it, you realize that the comfort Jesus offers is a pretty rare find. Every one of us comes to the Beatitudes with a past. We carry a certain amount of baggage with us when we move into this new way of living. Indeed, claiming that baggage, recognizing and owning up to it, is the point of the first two Beatitudes.

That baggage gets heavy, doesn't it? "*Un*comfortable" is the word that comes to mind. We've hauled around mountains of guilt and regret and self-loathing and shame and memories of failures past. Back in the old life, all we managed to do was add to the pile. It grew heavier and more burdensome with every passing day. No matter how much we cried, there was always something else to mourn.

When we escape to the Beatitudes, however, we get to unpack. Jesus stands beside us as we open each piece of baggage. Where there are sins, he takes them and says, "I'll carry those for you." Where there's guilt, he offers true forgiveness and the relief of release. In place of our shame, he gives us acceptance and love. For old habits and addictions, he gives us new power and fresh victories.

When Jesus says, ". . . for they will be comforted," he's speaking music to our ears. This is one of the sweetest, most welcome promises he makes. We're so hungry for comfort, so ready to lay down our burdens, that this alone should make our decision for us. Why go back to the troubles of an old life when, in Beatitude living, we can find *comfort?*

But wait! There's more! Jesus next makes the promise that Beatitude people "will inherit the earth." Is that the same thing as taking over the planet? Is Jesus promising disciples world domination? Hey, there might be something to these Beatitudes after all!

Jesus lifts this Beatitude right out of Psalm 37:11.

There, David speaks of the *present* blessings enjoyed by those who are yielded to God. Such people do not need to worry or fear. They enjoy safety and security in this life, confident that God is watching over them and taking care of them. The meek inherit not just a future heaven but a here-and-now earth.

I think Jesus is promising something similar here. Instead of seeing the Beatitudes as a religious layaway plan (obey now, get your reward later), Jesus may be telling us that the traits of a disciple bring their own, immediate rewards. Live out the Beatitudes and watch your relationships deepen and prosper. Live out the Beatitudes and discover in yourself a tangible sense of peace and joy. Live out the Beatitudes and witness real change taking place in your character and priorities and spirituality.

These are just a few of the ways in which the benefits of the Beatitudes flow to us in the present. God's blessings are

contemporary. We *are* (present tense) inheriting the earth.

That's one more reason for turning away from the old life and moving into the new. Back there, it felt like we had the world on our shoulders. With Jesus, it feels like we've got the world by the tail. Are you ready to make a commitment now?

Be patient. Jesus offers even more to those who walk his way.

In the fourth Beatitude, Jesus makes a promise that others, before and since, also have offered. Yet, in spite of all the people peddling it, it remains the most rare treasure in all the world. The Rolling Stones couldn't "get" any of it. Neither can most of their contemporaries. But people who love righteousness can,

. . . for they will be satisfied.

Here's an offer worth paying careful attention to. Jesus says that Beatitude living results in completion, contentment, gratification, fulfillment. Silly us. We thought such things came from driving the right car or indulging the right craving or making the right salary. We've listened to and believed every smooth talker with a "get-satisfied-quick" scheme. Our lives are littered with broken gimmicks and failed strategies—all promising to give us the satisfaction we crave.

Jesus says that only *righteousness* can result in satisfaction. For satisfaction, in the end, is not an attainment. It's a gift from God. It can never be mastered. It can only be received. Those who give their lives to God will be granted fullness in every aspect of life.

Not bad! Are you feeling tempted now? Jesus stands in the middle of the Beatitudes, inviting us to join him in a lifestyle full of promise and rich in blessings. Are you ready to make your decision?

Perhaps you need to see just a few more benefits before being fully convinced. "There's mercy here," says Jesus. People who live like this tap into the compassion of God. Where forgiveness is necessary, it will be granted. Where needs exist, they'll be met. When grace is required, it will be extended.

Oh, how we need that! How could you even think about turning back to what you came from? Why go back to the graceless, close-fisted, merciless world you inhabited before? Sure the Beatitudes are a challenge. They're all so new and mysterious. We're not sure where they'll lead. But doesn't the promise of mercy go a long way toward easing your doubts and making your decision?

"Do you want to see God?" asks Jesus finally. "Do you want to be called his child? *Here* is where that happens." Now all pretense of playing fair has vanished. Jesus pulls out the best treasures in the entire kingdom. These are his "closers"—the promises sure to seal the deal.

People who live the Beatitudes see God. They see his hand at work in their lives. They see his face in their prayers. They see his likeness growing within them. The Beatitudes are a door disciples enter into the presence of God. They're a lens that brings a distant God near. They're a certificate, authenticating the disciple's gazing rights. They're a seam between the physical and the spiritual, a crack that the invisible God can be seen through.

That's why you ought to screw up your courage and commit yourself to the Beatitude lifestyle. Seeing God is worth any risk or hazard there may be.

And to be called his child! To live so much like God that he recognizes a part of himself in you. To be known as a chip off the old block! To look like him more and more each day—as only true sons and daughters can.

If this doesn't cause you to jump to your feet and run to meet Jesus and his Beatitudes, if this does not persuade you to throw caution to the wind and embrace these daunting characteristics, if this doesn't make you see clearly the pettiness and futility of your old life . . . then go back. Turn around and walk away from him. Return to what's familiar and easy. Jesus offers it all here—if you don't want this, there's nothing more he can give you.

If these promises aren't enough, go back.

HAPPY ENDINGS

One girl lost her nerve. The remaining five young women made their trembling way into the town. They found a cellar that was hidden and relatively dry. They scrounged and scavenged for food and other necessities. They held each other during the day, too frightened to make a sound. They lived with the uncertainty, the imminent danger, and the daily possibility of failure.

A week passed. A month. They were continually hungry, commonly cold, constantly afraid. And then one morning they heard the shouts— "Americaners komme! Americaners komme!" Elizabeth Roth and her companions stumbled blinking into the light to watch a great river of men and equipment flowing through the streets of Essen.

The nightmare years were over. Their deliverers had come. Because they dared to go forward rather than back, they put themselves in a position where rescue was possible.

That's what Jesus asks of us as we sit with him on this mountainside and contemplate a different manner of living. He doesn't promise us a rose garden. He doesn't say there will be no hungry days, no uncertain times, no failures or dangers. There may be months or years when Jesus and his Beatitudes seem too demanding and require too much. There will be times when the best we can do is hang on to each other and put our hopes in the grace of God.

But one day, those who have the courage to venture into the unknown, who embrace the Beatitudes in spite of their fears and their questions will hear the cry, "Jesus comes! Jesus comes!" And we'll stumble blinking into his bright light and watch him return on clouds in the air.

Then Jesus will say to us, "Come, you who are blessed by my Father; take your inheritance, the kingdom prepared for you since the creation of the world."[4] He'll comfort us and wipe every tear. He'll give us heaven and earth and every other good thing. He'll fill the desires of our hearts and pour out his abundant mercy upon us. He'll lead us into the presence of his Father, where we will see God face to face and hear him call us his true children.

Because we dared to go forward rather than back, we'll find ourselves in a place where ultimate rescue is possible.

Maranatha! Even so, Lord Jesus. Come quickly.

CHAPTER ONE: THE ILLUS-TRATED DISCIPLE

1. In Matthew, there is a brief interlude between the calling of the first disciples and the Sermon on the Mount (4:23-25). Jesus preaches and heals during this period, but there are no recorded interactions with the disciples as a group. His first words to the assembled disciples (his first "teaching" words to them) occur in 5:3. Even at this point, Matthew Levi has yet to be called (an event that does not occur in Matthew until the ninth chapter) and the Twelve are not listed as a distinct group until 10:1-4. In Luke, the ordering of events is different, and the interlude between calling and teaching is even more dramatic. The first disciples are called beginning in 5:1 and Levi in 5:27. The Twelve are listed in 6:12-16. Jesus begins the "Sermon on the Plain" (including a truncated version of the Beati-tudes) in 6:20. But apart from the initial interactions with Peter and Levi, there is not a word addressed to the disciples until the sermon begins. Jesus speaks to and heals a leper, he has some unfortunate interactions with the Pharisees (three or four conflicts in the span of these few verses), he heals a paralytic and forgives his sins, he defends himself against critics, and meets and heals a man with a shriveled hand. But nothing is said to his disciples until he looks at them and says, "Blessed are you who are poor" (6:20). Luke is explicit that all of the apostles are present when Jesus speaks the Beatitudes.

2. I recognize that there is some discussion in the scholarly literature about which audience Jesus is really addressing here—the disciples or the crowds. Are these words intended for the masses or for a more select group who had already made commitments to him? Does Jesus shout this discourse or whisper it? Or does he do a little of both? In the sermon to follow, Jesus says a number of things that appear to be directed to a larger audience. What he says, for instance, about murder, adultery, divorce, and revenge was appropriate for everyone to hear. But some of what Jesus says in this sermon (especially near the beginning, in the first twenty verses) seems more appropriate for the disciples. It was Peter and his peers whom Jesus called salt of the earth and light of the world—not every Tom, Dick, and Joseph who happened to be within hearing range of these statements. In the same way, the Beatitudes seem more suited to the disciples than to the crowds. I am convinced Jesus whispered these sayings to the Twelve rather than bellowing them for benefit of the mob. Only later in the sermon does his atten-

tion shift from the disciples to the hangers on.

3. Matthew 5:2, emphasis added.
4. Matthew 5:3-10.
5. Galatians 1:7.

CHAPTER TWO: FATHER . . . CAN YOU SPARE A DIME?

1. Matthew 5:3.
2. William Barclay makes this point in *The Gospel of Matthew, Vol. 1*, in the *Daily Study Bible Series* (Philadelphia: Westminster Press, 1975), as does Fredrick Dale Bruner in *The Christbook: Matthew 1-12* (Waco: Word Books, 1987).
3. Barclay, p. 92.
4. Luke 18:14.
5. Matthew 21:31-32.
6. Matthew 18:3-6.
7. Mark 9:43-48.
8. Luke 18:24.
9. Luke 5:29-32.
10. Luke 7:36-50.
11. "Be Ye Perfect, More or Less," *Christianity Today,* 17 July 1995, pp. 38-41.
12. For an interesting account of Newton's life, read John Pollock's *Amazing Grace: The Dramatic Life Story of John Newton* (San Francisco: Harper & Row, 1981).
13. Brian Abel Ragen, "A Wretch Like Who?" *America*, 29 January 1994, pp. 8-11. I have adapted Ragen's basic points and much of his language in this segment.

CHAPTER THREE: COME MOURN WITH US

1. Matthew 5:4.
2. Richard C. Trench, *Synonyms of the New Testament* (Grand Rapids: Eerdmans, 1953).
3. Matthew 2:16-18.
4. John 11:31.
5. Mark 16:10.
6. Psalm 51:16-17.
7. I am indebted to John M. T. Barton's *Penance and Absolution* (New York: Hawthorn Books, 1961) for educating me on the sacrament of penance.

CHAPTER FOUR: THE MIGHTY MEEK

1. *The Tyndale Bible* (1525—the first English version translated directly from the Hebrew and Greek), the *Great Bible* (1539), the *King James Version* (1611), and the *Geneva Bible* (1560—the version familiar to Shakespeare and the Puritans) all used the word meek (or *meke*) in translating Matthew 5:5.
2. Ephesians 4:2, RSV.
3. Numbers 12:3, RSV.
4. Matthew 11:29, KJV.
5. I am grateful to D. Martyn Lloyd-Jones in *The Sermon on the Mount* for pointing this out to me.
6. Andrea Sachs, "From Prisoner to Preacher," *ABA Journal,* volume 79, May 1993, pp. 38-39. See also Garry Wills, "Born Again Politics," *New York Times Magazine,* 1 August 1976, pp. 8-9,48-49.
7. Richard Foster, *Celebration of Discipline: The Path to Spiritual Growth* (New York: Harper & Row, 1978), pp. 106-107.

CHAPTER FIVE: HUNGERING FOR GOD

1. Genesis 29:17.
2. Jacob wept when he first saw Rachel and claimed it was because she was family. I wonder if there was as much chemistry as kinship in his response.
3. Genesis 29:18.
4. Genesis 29:20.
5. Genesis 29:25.
6. Psalm 42:1-2.
7. Philippians 3:7-8.
8. Jeremiah 20:9.
9. Martin Luther, *The Sermon on the Mount.* In *Luther's Works,* edited by Jaroslav Pelikan, volume 21 (St Louis: Concordia, 1956), p. 27.
10. Martyn Lloyd-Jones, *Studies in the Sermon on the Mount,* Volume 1 (Grand Rapids: Eerdmans, 1959), p. 79.
11. Jeremiah 15:16.
12. Matthew 5:10-12. See also chapter 9.
13. Matthew 5:20.
14. Matthew 6:1-18.
15. Matthew 6:33.
16. Mark 9:24.

CHAPTER SIX: HAVE MERCY

1. Matthew 5:7.
2. Matthew 6:14.
3. Matthew 9:27-29; 20:29-34.
4. Matthew 15:21-22.
5. Matthew 17:14-15.
6. James 2:15-16.

7. Matthew 9:36; 14:14; 15:32.
8. Luke 10:30-37.
9. Specifically, they are "going down" from Jerusalem to Jericho. Jerusalem is built on a hill and both the city of Jerusalem and the temple itself are frequently called Mount Zion. In fact, Jerusalem is the highest point for miles around. The Bible always talks about traveling "up" to Jerusalem or "down" from Jerusalem. The road from Jerusalem to Jericho drops some 3,300 feet in elevation along its seventeen-mile route.
10. Mark 2:1-5.
11. Mark 5:22-34.
12. Luke 7:36-50.
13. Luke 6:6-11.
14. Luke 4:18-19.
15. Matthew 22:36-40.
16. Matthew 23:2.
17. You may want to read the following articles to learn more about this remarkable woman. Kenneth Woodward, "Little Sister of the Poor," *Newsweek,* 15 September 1997, pp. 70-74. Emily Mitchell, Jan McGirk, and Nina Biddle, "Saint of the Streets," *People Weekly,* 22 September 1997, pp. 158-161. Marci McDonald, "Death of a Saint," *Maclean's,* 15 September 1997, pp. 22-25.

CHAPTER SEVEN: THE REAL THING

1. Matthew 5:8.
2. The word translated "pure" in our English Bibles is the Greek word καθαρος. The following discussion traces how this word (and its cognates) is used in Scripture. Where Old Testament references are considered, the Septuagint (the Greek translation of the Old Testament) is in mind.
3. Matthew 23:26; 23:25; 8:2-3; 27:59 respectively—just to demonstrate the diverse uses of this term in Matthew's gospel.
4. Psalm 51:10.
5. 1 Timothy 5:22.
6. 2 Corinthians 7:1.
7. Psalms 24:3-4.
8. I'm grateful to John R. W. Stott for this insight in his book *The Message of the Sermon on the Mount* (Downers Grove, IL: InterVarsity, 1978), p. 49.
9. James addresses Christians who can't decide which side they are on. There are discrepancies between what they know and what they do, between their words and their actions. They harbor "bitter envy and selfish ambition" in their hearts (James 3:14), all the while denying the fact. They want to be on good terms with the world *and* with God. They are busy playing both ends against the middle. James will have none of it: "You adulterous people . . . Come near to God and he will come near to you. Wash your hands, you sinners, and purify your hearts, you double-minded" (James 4:4,8).

How do "double-minded" people "purify" their hearts? By making their hearts "single" once more; by deciding once and for all for God; by confessing their "sins to each other" and praying "for each other so that you may be healed" (James 5:16); by choosing an authentic Christian walk.

Paul, when talking to Timothy about how to conduct himself as a preacher of the gospel, contrasts a "pure heart" (1 Timothy 1:5) with false teachers who are plagued by insincerity and mixed motives. Paul links a "pure heart" with "a good conscience and a sincere faith," and encourages Timothy to open his life as an example to others. Throughout this book, Paul's emphasis is on the idea that there should be nothing hidden, no falseness or pretense, about the behavior of a minister of God. He should be pure (sincere) in heart.

See Matthew 23:25-28; Mark 7:1-23; and Luke 11:39-41 for examples of this same usage in the Gospels.
10. J. B. Phillips, *The New Testament in Modern English* (New York: Macmillan, 1958), p. 8.
11. William Barclay, *The Beatitudes and the Lord's Prayer for Everyman* (New York: Harper & Row, 1963), p. 81.
12. Genesis 2:25.
13. Genesis 3:10.
14. 2 Timothy 3:5.
15. Colossians 2:20–3:11.

CHAPTER EIGHT:
GIVE PEACE A CHANCE

1. Bruce Felton and Mark Fowler, *Felton and Fowler's Best, Worst, and Most Unusual* (New York: Gramercy, 1984), p. 110.
2. Isaiah 11:1-9.
3. Isaiah 9:6-7.
4. Genesis 3:15.
5. Revelation 19:11-15.
6. Luke 2:14.
7. Luke 2:34-35.
8. Ephesians 2:17.
9. John 14:27.
10. Mark 9:50.
11. Matthew 10:34. See also Luke 12:51.
12. Matthew 12:30; Luke 11:23.
13. Luke 9:62.
14. Matthew 23:13-33.
15. Mark 3:5.
16. John 2:15.
17. Jesus does ask us to love our enemies, but he assumes we *will* have enemies—people who do not like us very much, people who will not be at peace with us. See Matthew 5:43-47.
18. Luke 5:8.
19. Matthew 14:28-31.
20. Matthew 15:15-16.
21. Matthew 18:21.
22. Luke 5:8-10.
23. Matthew 14:28-31.
24. Matthew 15:17-20.
25. Matthew 16:22.
26. Matthew 17:1-8.
27. Matthew 26:40,55-56,69-75; John 18:10-11.
28. John 21:15-19.
29. Mark 10:35-40; Luke 9:52-55.
30. John 20:24-29.
31. John 6:5-7; 14:8-9.
32. Mark 8:14-21; 9:33-35; Luke 8:23-25.
33. James Hinkle and Tim Woodroof, *Among Friends* (Colorado Springs, CO: NavPress, 1989), pp. 121-122.
34. Romans 14:19.
35. Matthew 18:21-22.
36. Matthew 5:23-24; Luke 6:28-29; 17:3; 15:18.

CHAPTER NINE:
TO MARCH INTO HELL FOR A HEAVENLY CAUSE

1. Matthew 5:10.
2. John 5:16. Because Jesus was doing these things on the Sabbath, the Jews persecuted him.
3. John 15:21.
4. Matthew 23:29-31.
5. Jeremiah 20:1-8; 26:7-11; 38:1-6; 43:1-3.
6. The same can be said of the apostle Paul. Though Paul was occasionally abused by strangers in Asia Minor and Greece, he was hounded far more vehemently by people he knew and who knew him. It was his own countrymen who abused, slandered, and conspired to kill him on numerous occasions (Acts 9:23; 14:5,19; 17:5,13; 18:6; 19:9; 20:3; 23:12). A group of Jewish Christians actively accused Paul of preaching a false gospel, of falsely posing as an apostle of Jesus, and of being soft on sin. Some of his own converts, people he had preached to and lived with, said hurtful things about Paul and tried to undermine his ministry (see 2 Corinthians 10–11). Given a choice, Paul would have preferred a beating by an anonymous jailer in Philippi to the ridicule and insults heaped upon him by members of his own church.
7. See John 11:48.
8. 2 Timothy 3:12.
9. John 15:20. Although the immediate precedent of this pronoun is "world," Jesus is not referring only to lost Gentiles with this statement. By this point in John's gospel, anyone who does not accept Jesus and yield to his lordship (whether Jew or Gentile, religious or not) belongs to the world.

CHAPTER TEN:
PROMISES, PROMISES

1. William Manchester, *The Arms of Krupp* (Boston: Little, Brown, 1964), p. 585.
2. Job 5:17-18; Psalm 1:1-3; 41:1; 128:1-2; Proverbs 8:34-35; Jeremiah 17:7-8; James 1:12.
3. See Matthew 6:10,33; 11:11-12; 13:44-46; 25:34.
4. Matthew 25:34.

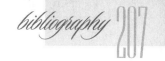

BOOKS CONSULTED ON THE BEATITUDES OR THE SERMON ON THE MOUNT

Barclay, William. *The Gospel of Matthew,* Volume 1 (Chapters 1-10) in *The Daily Study Bible Series.* Philadelphia: Westminster, 1958.

Barclay, William. *The Beatitudes and the Lord's Prayer for Everyman.* New York: Harper & Row, 1975.

Betz, Hans Dieter. *The Sermon on the Mount.* Minneapolis: Fortress, 1995.

Bonhoeffer, Dietrich. *The Cost of Discipleship.* New York: Macmillan, 1959.

Bruner, Fredrick Dale. *Matthew, a Commentary: Volume 1, The Christbook (Matthew 1-12).* Dallas: Word, 1987.

Carson, D. A. *The Sermon on the Mount: An Evangelical Exposition of Matthew 5-7.* Grand Rapids: Baker, 1978.

Cope, Mike. *Righteousness Inside Out: The Heart of the Problem and the Problem of the Heart.* Nashville: Christian Communication, 1988.

Fitch, William. *The Beatitudes of Jesus.* Grand Rapids, MI: Eerdmans, 1961.

Guelich, Robert A. *The Sermon on the Mount: A Foundation for Understanding.* Waco, TX: Word, 1982.

Hagner, Donald A. *Matthew 1-13.* Volume 33A in *Word Biblical Commentary Series.* Edited by Ralph P. Martin (ed. for New Testament). Dallas: Word, 1993.

Lloyd-Jones, D. Martyn. *Studies in the Sermon on the Mount,* Volume 1. Grand Rapids, MI: Eerdmans, 1976.

Lucado, Max. *The Applause of Heaven.* Dallas: Word, 1990.

Palmer, Earl F. *The Enormous Exception: Meeting Christ in the Sermon on the Mount.* Waco, TX: Word, 1986.

Seals, Thomas L. *The Sermon on the Mount for Modern Living.* Abilene, TX: Quality Publications, 1989.

Shelly, Rubel. *The Beatitudes: Jesus' Formula for Happiness.* Nashville, TN: Twentieth Century Christian, 1982.

Stott, John R. W. *Christian Counter-Culture: The Message of the Sermon on the Mount* in *The Bible Speaks Today Series.* Edited by J. A. Motyer and John R. W. Stott. Downers Grove, IL: InterVarsity, 1978.

TIM WOODROOF follows an almost genetic call to preach. Both his father and grandfather were in the ministry. Altogether, the three of them share over 120 years of preaching experience. Tim has served churches in Nebraska, Oregon, and (now) Nashville, Tennessee. He has written one other book for NavPress (*Among Friends: You Can Help Make Your Church a Warmer Place*) and is the author of numerous programs for adult education in churches.

Tim did his graduate work in psychology and theology, receiving an M.S. in clinical Psychology (from Texas A&M University) and a Ph.D. in Community and Human Resources (University of Nebraska). He narrowly avoided being awarded a M.Th. from the Harding Graduate School of Religion in Memphis by virtue of being so tired of school he could not bring himself to write yet another thesis.

Though Tim speaks for functions around the country, his primary love is the local church. Recently he and his family moved to Nashville to work with the Otter Creek Church. He and Julie have been married for twenty years. They have three (mostly) adorable children—Sarah, James, and Jonathan. Tim has notified us that he is booking speaking appointments only in places close to blue ribbon trout streams.